Engineering Ethics

includes

Human Values

M. Govindarajan
Formerly Assistant Professor
Department of Mechanical Engineering
Anna University, Chennai

S. Natarajan
Formerly Professor and Head
Department of Mechanical Engineering
Anna University, Chennai

V.S. Senthilkumar
Assistant Professor
Department of Mechanical Engineering
Anna University, Chennai

PHI Learning Private Limited
Delhi-110092
2025

In fond memory of ***Shri Asoke K. Ghosh*** *(October 1942 – February 2024), Founder Chairman and Managing Director of PHI Learning, whose vision endlessly inspires.*

The Legacy Continues....

Published by Pushpita Ghosh, PHI Learning Private Limited, Rimjhim House, 111, Patparganj Industrial Estate, Delhi-110092 and Printed by Multi Colour Services, I-45, DLF Industrial Area, Sector-32, Faridabad, Haryana-121003.

₹525.00

ENGINEERING ETHICS (includes Human Values)
M. Govindarajan, S. Natarajan and V.S. Senthilkumar

ISBN-978-81-203-2578-4 (Print Book)
ISBN-978-93-90464-34-0 (e-Book)

The export rights of the book are vested solely with the publisher.

To

The Lotus Feet of the Holy Mother

A Prayer

"I stretch it out to Thee with both arms
in a gesture of offering and I ask of Thee:

If my understanding is limited, widen it;
if my knowledge is obscure, enlighten it;
if my heart is empty of ardour, set it aflame;
if my love is insignificant, make it intense;
if my feelings are ignorant and egoistic,
give them the full consciousness in the Truth"!

On the Mother
by **K.R. Srinivas Iyengar**

Contents

Preface

Engineering Ethics, as a subject of study, owes its origin not only to the lack of ethics that led to the engineering disasters that have been recorded over a period of time but also to the day-to-day ethical behaviour that ought to be followed by engineering professionals. In the case of disasters, several factors were responsible—overconfidence (Titanic disaster), impatience (space shuttle Challenger explosion), negligence and poor maintenance (Bhopal Gas Tragedy). Most of the disasters could have been prevented if the necessary code of ethics was observed. In order to cut down on the number of errors, both human and mechanical, many codes of ethics were established. The main purpose of these ethical codes is to ensure public safety.

Ethics presupposes understanding of human nature and values. Values provide each one of us with a unique, personal, and moral template that we use to assess the intentions and actions of others and ourselves and the importance of the likely outcome of these various actions and reactions. By values, we mean an in-built mechanism which distinguishes the right from the wrong. Right or wrong should be interpreted only in the context of the social environment in which a person lives. There is a growing concern about deteriorating values because deviation from accepted values threatens the stability of society. Excessive technological growth has created an environment in which life has become physically and mentally unhealthy. The quality of work-life in any organization is greatly influenced by the ethical and moral values prevalent in that organization. The ethical quality of managerial decision-making can be improved through a full understanding and internalization of the doctrine of *karma*. All decisions depend critically on the purity of mind of the decision-maker.

There are five system values and many sub-values, or virtues that come from these. They contain all that makes a human being noble, caring, and kind. The Five Universal Values from which the other values and virtues stem are Right Conduct (using the tool of the body), Peace (using the tool of the mind), Truth (using the power of discrimination and intellect), Love (using the power of energy), and Non-Violence (awakening to the Spirit within). Indian ethos asserts that the spirit must lead matter and not vice versa. Since all minds and all lives are interconnected, a respectful attitude of honesty, help, care and encouragement are not only the best policy but the only policy in management. These ideas are explained in detail in Chapter 0.

The material for the book is taken from different sources like scriptural writings, the contemporary writings on professional ethics, and the Internet. Whatever presented is only 'received knowledge'. The objectives of the book are to introduce the readers to the ethical concepts that are relevant to resolving moral issues in engineering, to impart reasoning and analytical skills needed to apply ethical concepts to engineering decisions, to identify the moral issues involved in both management and engineering areas, and to provide an understanding of the interface between social, technological and natural environments.

Chapter 1 presents the fundamentals of ethics, starting from the Indian ethos and goes on to explain the various concepts of engineering ethics. Deontological, consequentialist, and virtue approaches to the study of ethical behaviour are explained. Engineering as a profession is discussed by comparison with Medicine and Law. The pros and cons of social involvement of business are explained. The code of ethics and how to solve ethical conflicts have also been covered. Chapter 2 deals with moral reasoning and ethical theories. Theories of right action using the concept of utilitarianism, cost-benefit analysis, and duty and right ethics are also discussed. Three kinds of inquiries—normative, conceptual, and factual—are explained. Types of moral dilemmas, various models of moral development and value-based ethics are dealt with. Engineering as social experimentation is discussed in Chapter 3. The engineers' responsibility for safety and risk is explained in Chapter 4. Collegiality and loyalty are discussed in Chapter 5. Also discussed are the rights and responsibilities of engineers in an organizational setting. Global issues like environmental ethics, weapons development, and Intellectual Property Rights (IPRs) are detailed in Chapter 6. The final chapter deals with ethical audit.

Review questions and four case studies are provided to sharpen the analytical skills of the students.

Teaching a course on Professional Ethics is difficult for two reasons. First, understanding the subject matter is difficult as it is somewhat amorphous. The teacher should have a good grasp of the principles of general ethics before branching out into engineering ethics. Secondly, the teacher should have good vocabulary and presentation skills. Hence, fluency in oral presentation and the ability to impart reasoning and analytical skills needed to apply ethical concepts to engineering decisions are emphasized.

Writing a book is often a tedious job. It requires lot of reading, writing, typing and editing. We acknowledge with thanks the excellent support given by Mrs. Prabha in typing the manuscript and Mr. S. Muthukrishnan for his help in page layout and in improving the general getup.

I thank Prentice-Hall of India for bringing out a sleek edition of the book.

Any constructive comments for improving the contents will be greatly appreciated.

M. Govindarajan
S. Natarajan
V.S. Senthilkumar

Chapter 0

Human Values

"udyamam sahasam dhairyam buddhih saktih parakramah sadete yatra vartante tatra devah sahayakrt"

—a Sanskrit verse

(Where the six qualities of right effort, enterprise, courage, know-how, resources, and the ability to reshuffle priorities reside, there God lends a hand.)

Values mean an in-built mechanism which distinguishes the right from the wrong. Right or wrong should not be interpreted in any absolute metaphysical sense and should be interpreted only in the context of the social environment in which a person lives, moves and acts. There is a growing concern for deteriorating values because deviation from accepted values threatens the stability of society. Irrespective of religious diversity, there exists a remarkable degree of agreement about values such as honesty, integrity, compassion, tolerance and selflessness.

Values serve the process of 'becoming', in the sense of transformation of the level of consciousness to purer, higher levels. Skills are concerned with the method of 'doing', in the sense of speed, dexterity, efficiency, etc. Values are, therefore, essentially subjective while skills are objective. While education is more germane to values, training relates more closely to skills.

Values provide us with a unique, personal, and moral template that we use subconsciously to assess and judge the intentions and actions of others and ourselves, and the importance of the likely outcome of various actions and reactions. Many of our values are derived from the myths about ourselves, our culture and our place in the universe (our personal cosmology), which make up the largely unconscious framework within which we live and have our being. They are the pragmatic outcome of what we have acepted as true answers (without much critical consideration) to the fundamental questions posed by philosophy, ethics and religion. And for most of us, the personal cosmology is derived far more from intuition and faith than from logic.

Values are something we qualify as good and are prepared to set as our goals in life. Furthermore, we usually do not include satisfaction of our physical needs in the concept, even though we appreciate it and have to achieve it all the time, often simply in order to survive. It would be fair to say that the concept of values describes that part of our goals which is not immediately necessary for survival. When two different goals come into conflict, we call for a higher goal, or a principle, or a value, which we choose to resolve the conflict. This is the problem of ethics.

Human Values can be classified as:

(i) Values relating to an individual (such as 'good' and 'bad') which, when considered carefully, can be related primarily to the person.
(ii) Values, where there is normally an element of consensus implied, as in terms such as 'fair', 'decent', and 'tolerant'.
(iii) Values relating primarily to things in the sense of 'fitting' (that is to say, appropriate for their purpose), such as a 'good' pen, a 'good' computer, and a 'good' tennis racquet. This can, in a way, be taken to include the others because we are concerned with the extent to which human values are fitting for their purpose.

With regard to the first two types of values, there are two separate and important aspects. First, how does each culture establish its current, commonly accepted values? Second, how does each person acquire the values that are unique for him or her, given that all such individual values must inevitably be strongly coloured and, indeed, broadly determined by the culture in which he or she was born and bred?

Management by values highlights the concept of 'self' in man. It is to be understood that the creative energies of human beings are derived from and rooted in the Supreme Creative Intelligence. The key to cooperation and teamwork lies in the progressive assimilation of the reality that the same soul dwells in all. The ethical quality of managerial decision-making can be improved through a full understanding and internalization of the doctrine of *karma.* Effective leadership style requires an understanding of the three *gunas—sattwa* (purity and righteousness), *rajas* (aversion and selfishness), and *tamas* (ignorance and laziness). All decisions depend critically on the purity of mind of the decision-maker. The virtues held in high esteem are simplicity, sacrifice, renunciation, and compassion.

0.1 DEGENERATION IN VALUES

Business management in the Western world has been heavily influenced by the same philosophy that underlies consumerism. This has resulted in environmental problems, over-consumption of raw materials and a society without values. The tendency to be more concerned with consumption than with creation has affected the social structures on which society is based.

This can be seen most clearly in the dissolution of the traditional family. Rapid degeneration of values reaches a critical stage when a catastrophic change becomes inevitable. The forces that create and hasten this process of degeneration are widespread—corruption, crime against the weak, violence, destruction, intolerance, discourtesy, and general vulgarity all around. These are but manifestations of the brutalization, the dehumanization of the individual in the society. It is more likely to happen in a society polarized between a privileged few who have everything and a growing majority who have little or nothing. The larger the number of deprived individuals, the greater the degree of alienation and the desire to hurt the society and the greater also the resentment at continued deprivation and neglect. In such a society, deterioration of values takes place at both ends. The rich indulge in their insatiable greed without scruples and the larger number feel justified to employ any means to satisfy their unfulfilled basic needs. Thus, the most powerful external forces likely to erode cherished human values are abject poverty and glaring inequality.

0.2 HOLISTIC CODE OF LIVING

On the other hand, the Indian ethos has stressed just the opposite—'give' rather than 'take'. The virtues held in high esteem have been simplicity and sacrifice, renunciation and compassion. All our legendary heroes symbolize these values. These were instilled constantly through the teacher, the *guru*. In our time, Tagore and Gandhiji were the last apostles of these values in a holistic code of living. They believed in the means being ethical. This may lead to a different end, namely maximum contentment with the minimum of material possessions—a value close to the Indian ethos but antithetical to modern Western beliefs. As far as growth is concerned, the corporate bodies have the largest potential for distortion of values. Institutions are guided by individuals at the helm, the chief executives or MDs. Therefore, firstly, a programme of sensitization at this level is necessary. Secondly, at the level of the individual, education directed towards value formation and management of the self has to be formally imparted at the school level and at work.

0.3 UNIVERSAL VALUES

There are five system values and many sub-values or virtues that come from these. They contain all that makes a human being noble, caring, and kind.

0.3.1 Right Conduct (Using the tool of the body)

Every action is preceded by thought. If the thought is unselfish, the action will be good for oneself and others. Right conduct is concerned with maintenance of the body to serve us in performing the tasks of life. The importance of exercise, such as gymnastics, yoga and sports combined with good rest, is emphasized. Good thoughts and good company are essential for healthy and well-balanced development.

0.3.2 **Peace** (Using the tool of the mind)

When our will power is sufficiently strong to enable us to discern the differences between real needs and superfluous desires, we cease to be driven by the urge to own more and more things. Inner agitation stops and we are peaceful. When there is peace in the individual, there will be peace in the family. When there is peace in the family, there will be peace in the community. In order to learn, self-esteem, calmness and freedom from anxiety are necessary.

0.3.3 **Truth** (Using the power of discrimination and intellect)

The desire to know truth has prompted mankind to ask some of the great questions such as: Who am I? What is the purpose of life? How can I know my inner self/God/the Creator of the universe? How can I live fully in the present moment? Learning to speak the truth is a first and vital step in the formation of a strong character. Voicing untruth is an anti-social act and causes confusion in the minds of both the speaker and listener and leads to anti-social behaviour. Telling lies hurts ourselves as well as others in a subtle, but very real way. One great distinction between human-kind and the rest of the animal kingdom is the ability to choose how to behave, rather than just to follow the low instincts (the law of the jungle). A human being is also able to recognize past, present and future to take note of changes occurring over time.

0.3.4 **Love** (Using the power of energy)

Love is not an emotion affected by the sub-conscious mind but is a spontaneous, pure reaction of the heart. It is the power of love, which causes one person to wish happiness for another and take pleasure in his or her well being. A beneficial energy (love) is directed towards the other person. As the energy flows through our own body first, it also enhances our own health. Love is unconditional, positive, regard for the good of another. It is giving and unselfish. Love is essential if children are to grow up healthy in mind and body. Love is the unseen undercurrent binding all the four values.

0.3.5 **Non-violence** (Awakening to the spirit within)

Non-violence can be described as universal love. When truth is glimpsed through intuition, love is activated. Love is giving, rather than grasping. This results in non-violence, i.e. the non-violation of the natural laws which create harmony with the environment. Non-violence relates to the spiritual universal aspect of being. Living in a way that causes as little harm as possible to oneself, other people, animals, plants and the planet, is a sign of a well-integrated and well-balanced personality.

0.4 FUNDAMENTAL VALUES

Indians have developed four fundamental values about human life which they have practiced throughout the ages.

1. Essential divinity inherent in all life (respect to God in all human beings).
2. The presence of divine motherhood in all women (respect to the divine mother in all women).
3. Religion is the manifestation of the divinity already in man. The plurality of religion is only on the surface. At the spiritual core, there is an essential unity of all of them (respect to different religions as different ways to manifest the divinity within).
4. Civilization is the manifestation of divinity in man. That society is the most civilized where the highest truths become practical. The end of all work is to bring out the divine in ourselves by serving the divine in others.

0.5 HOLISTIC VISION

Indian ethos asserts that the spirit must lead matter and not vice-versa. The 'left brain' activities of reason, accumulation of wealth, and dynamism must be guided by the 'right-brain' activities of sacrifice, love and holistic actions. Roosevelt's dynamism and Einstein's brain must be combined with and guided by Buddha's compassion for all, in order to avoid a tragedy of Hiroshima. Tata's wealth-generating capacity was inspired by Vivekananda's holistic vision, ushering in the great welfare-based industry in India.

Indians discovered in every human being, irrespective of caste, creed or nationality, the potentiality of the infinite. A human being is not a "political animal" as Aristotle thought, nor a "tool-making animal" as Benjamin Franklin thought and an "economic animal" as Alvin Toffler thought. Any service offered to him or her should, therefore, be a service offered to bring out the essential Christ-Buddha nature and infinite excellence dormant in him or her. The second truth that the Indians discovered is the essential unity of existence. It is a holistic universe where at a deeper level of an all-pervading consciousness, everything in the world is interconnected. It is on the basis of the holistic vision that Indians have developed the work-ethos of life. They found that all works, be it physical or mental, management, leadership, administration, have to be directed towards a single purpose—the manifestation of the essential divinity in man by working for the good of all beings.

0.6 QUALITY OF LIFE

Excessive technological growth has created an environment in which life has become physically and mentally unhealthy. The quality of work life in any organization is greatly influenced by the ethical and moral values prevalent in that organization. However, a number of business and industrial enterprises tend to disregard the importance of such values. One can see the result of this in India, where there are definite signs of deterioration in the ethical and moral standards of the people, practically, in all walks of life.

SOURCES

My humble *pranams* to the authors of the following books:

1. Biswanath Ghosh, *Ethics in Management and Indian Ethos*, Vikas Publishing House, 2005.
2. Swami Jitamananda, *Indian Ethos for Management*, Ramakrishna Ashrama, Rajkot, 1996.
3. *Bagavatgita*
4. Web Resource: Sri Satya Sai, *Teaching Human Values in Education*
5. *Complete works of Swami Vivekananda*
6. *The Gospel of Sri Ramakrishna* by *M.*

Chapter 1

Understanding Ethics

Business Ethics deal with the desired norms of behaviour that pertain to commercial transactions. A manager with personal integrity is more likely to make ethical decisions for the organization than one without such integrity. It is a common phenomenon, though it looks paradoxical, that while many individual businessmen are extremely religious in their private lives, in their business, they resort to unethical behaviour and hardly take account of the extent of human suffering that their actions might cause to society. However, a good business manager who is aware of public (consumer) interest, professional interest and organizational interest, will constantly endeavour to act in accordance with law and ethics.

The increased interest in business ethics in India is no doubt related to the sordid events of the past few years in the public affairs of the country. The nexus between business, crime and politics has led many to believe that the country is on the verge of ruin unless drastic reforms are put into place in all areas, including business.

1.1 ETHICS—ACTION ORIENTED

Ethics in business includes values governing commercial transactions not only among persons and among organizations but also among persons within organizations and political processes that regulate such transactions. The chain of cause and effect between behaviour and consequences is often long and not always visible. This causal chain is fraught with uncertainty at every link, which can result in varying consequences and can also result from varied moral values. It must be noted that:

1. Ethical norms emerge from self discovery by people who have several subtle ways to integrate social cohesion with self-realization.
2. In spite of vast differences in the context of different societies across the world and across time, there are remarkable similarities in these ethical norms. Some have greater applicability in some situations than in others.

3. It must be recognized that even while pursuing profits, the way business is conducted affects people all around in a variety of ways. It is of prime ethical importance that such consequences are fully understood by the managers.
4. The appeal to social cohesion can often be misused by the power structure to exploit the poor and the underprivileged.
5. Business situations constantly call upon managers to innovate technically and managerially to ensure that the outcome of their actions is for the good of all. Therefore, much of business ethics is merely being technically competent and resourceful.
6. In the hierarchical layers of ethical responsibility, the accountability of one level cannot be a substitute for accountability of another level. Thus, every individual has an ethical responsibility and accountability, which he cannot pass on to his superiors or subordinates, or to his organization. Similarly, organizations cannot push their responsibility to individuals.
7. There is much to be gained in ethical living by a spontaneous bonhomie than by philosophical arguments. Ethics is a matter of action and not of theoretical hair-splitting. The *summum bonum* of ethical education is experience and sensitization, and not what is given in rule books.

1.2 ETHICAL VISION

The whole purpose of religion and philosophy is to give us that which is inspiring, elevating and constructive. If we have ideals we must express them in our lives. These are the ideals of *karma yoga*, the great Indian system of right action. It proclaims that religion is not for the man who is inactive. On the contrary, it holds that the man who is active and energetic, who is constantly doing something in the world, has just as much right to enter the kingdom of heaven as the hermit who is closeted in his hermitage and absorbed in prayer. The main secret is to learn to work without attachment. Attachment to something makes us demand, while love unfolds the capacity for giving. Our physical constitution is largely dependent on the mind and the mind is dependent on the thought–force. Hence, when our thought is connected with some noble motive, it refreshes us. Those who are sincere, pure-hearted, true lovers of their fellowmen never hurt any one by thought, word or deed. The power of right thinking must be awakened; that is the first step. We all think; but thought is of two kinds—one is *constructive*: it uplifts man to great heights; the other is *destructive*, it degrades and, instead of helping, proves to be a great drawback. Yet the same mind is used for both. It is said in one of the Upanishads: "This mind is the cause of bondage and of liberation for all human beings. If attached to the world, it becomes bound; if freed from the world, that is liberty." How is it that the same mind can play such a double part? Because the mind can either go downward or it can go upward, whichever way we choose to direct it. It is ready to serve us and lead us onward; and if we neglect it, it will bind us and draw us back to the brute plane. Therefore, we cannot afford to disregard this important factor; for right thought is the flywheel of this great machine of human life and unless it revolves properly, the machine can do nothing. It may even be destroyed; if we are not discriminative. We may make mistakes that will prove our ruin. In the *Upanishads*, this body has been compared to a chariot, the senses are the horses, the mind, the reins, the intellect, the driver, and the Self who dwells within is the Lord of the chariot. Unless the horses are well controlled and the reins firmly held, unless the driver is intelligent, the chariot may be thrown off into the ditch and destroyed.

1.3 INDIAN ETHOS

Spiritual empiricism (the inner world of verifiable spiritual experience) has two intellectually allied alternatives: logical positivism and materialist empiricism. Each of these alternatives has a drawback. Whatever works in the sense-related domain of the immediate and visible seems to be its keynote. This is moral pragmatism. Classical Indian or Vedantic thought will be the principal source for this comparison and contrast.

1. It is still generally a taboo in India for lovers or spouses to kiss or embrace each other in public places.
2. Showing respect to parents, elders, superiors, teachers, in ways that differ very slightly is a uniform feature of Indian society.
3. The notion of marriage as a lifelong bond of mutual fidelity is still a dominant characteristic across all segments of Indian society.
4. In no Indian homes (barring those of a few pseudo-Western families) is a child made to sleep alone in order to protect it from the so-called dependence on parents. The point to be made is that when we think of Indian culture, uniformity in many vital respects keeps pace with diversity in others.
5. Even if the disputed theory of Aryan infiltration into India were accepted, it must still be remembered that the Vedas, Upanishads, the Smritis, the Puranas, and so on, blossomed only on Indian soil and were not brought over from the supposed original homes of the Aryans. So, although one might or might not agree that there is no one Indian culture, it is more important to understand and accept that there is indeed one Indian ethos deeply rooted in the Indian psyche.

1.4 ETHICS DEFINED

Ethics is defined as "the discipline dealing with what is good and bad and with moral duty and obligation". Thus, personal ethics has been referred to as "the rules by which an individual lives his or her personal life", and accounting ethics pertains to "the code that guides the professional conduct of accountants". Business Ethics is concerned "with truth and justice and has a variety of aspects such as the expectation of society, fair competition, advertising, public relations, social responsibilities, consumer autonomy, and corporate behaviour in the home country as well as abroad". Ethics is the study of the characteristics of morals. Ethics also deals with the moral choices that are made by each person in their relationship with other persons.

1.4.1 Engineering Ethics

Engineering ethics constitutes the rules and standards governing the conduct of engineers in their role as professionals. Engineering ethics encompasses the more general definition of ethics, but applies it more specifically to situations involving engineers in their professional lives. Thus, engineering ethics is a body of philosophy indicating the ways that engineers should conduct themselves in their professional capacity.

1.4.2 Ethical Decisions

Ethical decisions are not just decisions about the best way to meet a given brief or objective. They are concerned specifically with the quality of our decisions—with justice, with equity, with the consequences for all affected by the decision, and with the personal and collective responsibilities which lie beyond the contractual obligations into which we enter. We each develop a personal value system influenced by the social and cultural norms of our environment. These systems change continually as exposure to ever-wider experience modifies our attitudes.

1.4.3 Science of Ethics

The science of ethics addresses issues having both moral and practical significance. Decisions are not simply reactive, such as choosing which bus to catch, but involve concepts of study and responsibility, and of conflicts between rival goods or ills. Reflections upon the ethical significance and correctness of any situation require the use of judgemental reason which is not always familiar to engineers, fine-tuned as they are to the use of deductive logic and the pursuit of the 'correct' answer to any technical problem.

1.4.4 Nature of Ethical Problems

Ethical problems rarely have a single readily deducted solution. They deal in shades of meaning, uncertainty, doubt and complex relationships. They are part of an ethical continuum whose components are inextricably linked with one another and where a holistic view is needed. There is indivisibility in the continuum. Personal values cannot be separated from societal or professional values although it may be possible to reflect upon particular aspects to develop a comprehensive moral attitude. It is not possible to deal in precise rules and regulations, only to suggest guidelines. These guidelines give ethical behaviour its special place in maintaining the quality of life in communities.

1.4.5 Ethical Thinking

The study of ethics can be of two ways:

1. Ethics involves the discipline of systematic enquiry into moral norms or standards of behaviour and their underlying values and justification. It can help us understand and justify these values.
2. Applied ethics looks into the ways in which moral value (that which is valuable for the good of the environment and its inhabitants) can be applied to particular areas of concern such as business. Applied ethics reminds us that while the discipline of ethics may be treated as separate from other disciplines (such as mathematics or economics) when it comes to practice, the ethical dimensions is a fundamental part of all judgements and decisions. What becomes important then is the development of 'ethical thinking', which is a part of the decision-making process.

1.5 APPROACHES TO ETHICAL BEHAVIOUR

There are different ways of thinking about ethical behaviour. There are situations where two or more values, rights or obligations conflict with each other and a choice has to be made.

1.5.1 Deontological Theories

Deontology is the study of the nature of duty and obligations. Deontological theories see good as something that is self-evident and can be summed up in general rules which apply to all (it is wrong to kill). In this theory, the action of killing is always wrong. It breaks the basic rule of respect for life. Moral good is discovered through reasoned reflection. This approach is concerned primarily with the quality of an action, with the means of achieving a desired end. This approach has more of a religious undertone. The deontological theories assume the reasonableness of human beings, i.e. they are capable of seeing what is good. Ironically, deontological theories rely upon *consequentialist considerations* to justify themselves. Respect for life, for instance, is justified ultimately by the survival of the self, the community, and even the species.

1.5.2 Consequentialist Theories

Consequentialist theories (concerned with outcomes) see good as defined not by the action, but by the consequence. In this theory, killing another human being may be morally good, provided it gives rise to some greater good. For example, it has been argued that the deaths caused by the first atom bomb were morally acceptable because the consequence was to save far more lives through the consequent earlier ending of the war. One particular form of this theory, *utilitarianism*, sees good as being defined by the maximization of good consequences—the greatest good for the greatest number. This theory states that we can know what is good only when we have fully understood the context. This is also known as *teleological approach*.

The consequentialist approach ignores the importance of intention and motive in any ethical judgement. It also runs the danger of the ends justifying any means and even of denying the rights of minorities. In deciding between different options there has to be some understanding of what constitutes good in the first place.

1.5.3 Virtue

From the viewpoint of virtue (which implies high moral standards), good is found neither in the act nor in its consequence, but in the character of the moral agent. Such an approach stresses that no rule can give guidance in every situation and that we cannot effectively weigh up all the consequences. Thus, we need to develop the capacities to deal with each situation as it arises. This demands the development of personal or professional virtues, qualities that enable the person to be good and that spur him to do good. The principles implicit in the concept of individual virtue rightly emphasize the importance of not simply deciding what is good but of actually achieving ends that are good. Any virtue itself depends upon some prior definition of what is good.

1.5.4 Fundamental Virtues

The development of a personal value system results in 'moral maturity'—a state in which the individual has developed the capacity to take responsibility for ethical decision-making. It involves a moral freedom, the freedom both to see and to do one's duty. This implies a 'virtuous' person. The importance of virtues in ethical practice is clear. It is said that there are four fundamental virtues (Plato's Divine Virtues). They are:

- Wisdom
- Temperance
- Fortitude
- Justice.

Wisdom. Wisdom is an openness to the truth in all aspects of existence. It is closely related to the skills of listening and being still. It is crucial for avoiding premature judgement, and for achieving creative planning.

Temperance. Temperance is essentially the quality of moderation, balance and self-control. It does not preclude having fun but simply ensures that the person is not controlled by passions such as anger or fear, which tend to get in the way of good judgement. It is good to be well or even-tempered.

Fortitude. Fortitude looks to the quality of courage and resilience. It enables a person to make better decisions and to stand against the pressures and challenges that might corrupt judgement.

Justice. Justice is the quality of even judgement which enables equal treatment of all parties. It requires an awareness of right and wrong, and hence the acceptance of some code of standards.

The different virtues are interrelated. There is an essential unity of the virtues. We may perhaps have one virtue more fully developed and understood than others, but there is no doubt that all are essential to each other. Honesty is important for faith or trust to develop, fortitude for temperance, and so on. The concept of teamwork can be built upon the virtues of the different members accepting that it is rare to find someone with all the virtues fully developed. While individual value systems are clearly different, the development of morals is essentially a social process involving continual reflection and development based on experience and the accepted norms of a particular society. These range from the school and work environment to the influence of religious organizations, professional organizations and social groups. These are all related to more general and cultural value systems.

1.6 VARIOUS CONNOTATIONS OF ENGINEERING ETHICS

The word 'ethics' (like the word "morals") has several distinct although related meanings. Corresponding to them are various additional meanings of the expression "Engineering Ethics".

1. Ethics is an activity and an area of inquiry. It is the activity of understanding moral values, resolving moral issues and justifying moral judgements as well as the discipline or area of study resulting from the activity. Engineering ethics, accordingly, is an activity and discipline aimed at understanding the moral values that ought to guide engineering practice, resolving moral issues in engineering and justifying moral judgements concerning engineering.
2. When we speak of ethical problems, issues and controversies, we mean to distinguish them from non-moral problems. Here the word "ethical" marks a contrast between moral questions as well as questions of political, legal and artistic nature. Engineering ethics, in this sense, would refer to the set of specifically moral problems and issues related to engineering.
3. Sometimes the word "ethics" is used to refer to the particular set of beliefs, attitudes, and habits that a person or group displays concerning morality. Thus we speak of the Greek ethics, the German work ethics

the ethics of Martin Luther King. Jr. the civil rights leader, and the ethics of Mahatma Gandhi. In doing so, we are referring to the actual outlook of people on moral issues. Engineering ethics would therefore be the currently accepted codes and standards of conduct endorsed by various groups of engineers and engineering societies.

4. The word "ethics" and its grammatical variants can be used as synonyms for "morally correct". For example, people's actions and conduct can be spoken of as either ethical (right, good or permissible) or unethical (immoral), and individuals can be evaluated as ethical (decent, having moral integrity) or unethical (unscrupulous). In this usage, engineering ethics amounts to the set of justified moral principles of obligation, rights and ideals that ought to be endorsed by those engaged in engineering. Enunciating such principles and applying them to concrete situations is the central goal of the discipline of engineering ethics.

To take an example, "moral" rather than "ethical" is commonly used to describe sexually virtuous conduct, while "ethical" is preferred when referring to professionally virtuous conduct. Some would also say that "ethical" misdeeds are those that call for prosecution in civil court while "moral" misdeeds land one in criminal court and truly spoil reputations.

1.7 WHY STUDY ENGINEERING ETHICS?

Several notorious cases that have received a great deal of media attention in the past few years have led engineers to be increasingly aware of their professional responsibilities. These cases have led to an awareness of the importance of ethics within the engineering profession as engineers realize how their technical work has far-reaching impact on society. The work of engineers can affect public health and safety and can influence business practices and even politics. One result of this increase in awareness is that nearly every major corporation now has an "ethics office" that has the responsibility to ensure that employees have the ability to express their concerns about issues such as safety and corporate business practices in a way that will yield results and won't result in retaliation against the employees. Ethics offices also try to foster an ethical culture that will help to head off ethical problems in a corporation before they start. However, many times, the ethical problems encountered in engineering practice are very complex and involve conflicting ethical principles.

1.8 PERSONAL AND BUSINESS ETHICS

In discussing engineering ethics, it is important to make a distinction between personal ethics and professional or business ethics although there is not always a clear boundary between the two. Personal ethics deals with how we treat others in our day-to-day lives. Many of these principles are applicable to ethical situations that occur in business and engineering. However, professional ethics often involves choices on an organizational level rather than a personal level. Many of the problems will seem different because they involve relationships between two corporations, between a company and the government, or between corporations, companies and groups of individuals. Frequently, these types of relationships pose problems that are not encountered in personal ethics.

1.9 ETHICS AND THE LAW

The practice of engineering and business is governed by many laws on the international, federal, state, and local levels. Many of these laws are based on ethical principles although many are purely of a practical, rather than a philosophical nature. There is also a distinction between what is legal and what is ethical. Many things that are legal could be considered unethical. For example, designing a process that releases a known toxic, but unregulated substance into the environment is probably unethical although it is legal. Conversely, just because something is illegal does not mean that it is unethical. For example, there might be substances that were once thought to be harmful, but have now been shown to be safe, that you wish to incorporate into a product. If the law has not caught up with the latest scientific findings, it might be illegal to release these substances into the environment, even though there is no ethical problem with doing so. As an engineer, you are always minimally safe if you follow the requirements of the applicable laws. But in engineering ethics, we seek to go beyond the dictates of the law. Our interest is in areas where ethical principles conflict and there is no legal guidance for how to resolve the conflict.

1.10 ETHICS AND DESIGN PROBLEMS

The essence of engineering practice is the design of products, structures, and processes. The design problem is stated in terms of specifications: A device must be designed, which meets the criteria for performance, aesthetics, and price. Within the limits of these specifications, there are many "correct" solutions. There will, of course, be some solutions that are better than others in terms of higher performance or lower cost. Frequently, there will be two (or more) designs that are very different, yet perform identically. For example, a competing automobile manufacturer may design a car to meet the same market niche, yet each manufacturer's solution to the problem will be somewhat different. In engineering design, there is no unique correct answer. Ethical problem solving shares these attributes with engineering design. Although there will be no unique correct solution to most of the problems, there will be a range of solutions that are clearly right, some of which are better than others. There will also be a range of solutions that are clearly wrong. There are other similarities between engineering ethics and engineering design. Both apply a large body of knowledge to the solution of a problem and both involve the use of analytical skills. So, although the nature of the solutions to the problems in ethics will be different from those in most engineering cases, approaches to the problems and the ultimate solution will be very similar to those in engineering practice.

1.11 DUTIES AND RIGHTS

Ethical meaning can be considered through the concepts of duties and rights. It has been said that duties are axiomatic, while obligations are working hypotheses.

- Duties are offered unconditionally. They tend to be promissory and open-ended, such as the general duty owing to humanity.
- Obligations are based upon contractual relationships and are specific. Non-fulfillment of the obligation can lead to the end of the relationship.
- Rights are basically freedoms which enable the individual to fulfill important human needs such as family support or education. The precise list of human rights is a matter of debate.

1.11.1 Morality and Law

Traditionally, rights are divided into (a) moral rights argued for, on the basis of need, and (b) legal rights which are recognized and protected by law. This raises questions about the relationship between morality and law. The two are closely related, as would be expected, since they share key concepts such as justice, rights, rules and responsibility. The two areas are logically distinct. Law and legal justice are defined in terms of the procedural rules of the legal system. The law does not decide what ought to be legal or what the criteria of responsibility ought to be. Morality can provide a critique of the law and can argue for ways in which the law might be changed or interpreted, but the law cannot determine morality. Much greater flexibility is possible in an ethically sound society, in which just exchanges can take place without the need for restricting regulations, providing always that the mores are such that an excess of liberalism does not turn to unbridled license. Ethical decisions are concerned with the 'goodness' of things, or the 'rightness' of actions. Engineers' decisions have both a moral and a practical significance. These are decisions which are almost entirely practical, like opening an umbrella in the rain, or filling up the car with petrol.

1.12 WHAT IS A PROFESSION?

The attributes of a profession include:

1. The work requires sophisticated skills, the use of judgement, and the exercise of discretion. Also, the work is not routine and is not capable of being mechanized.
2. Membership in the profession requires extensive formal education, not simply practical training or apprenticeship.
3. The public allows special societies or organizations that are controlled by members of the profession to set standards for admission to the profession, to set standards of conduct for members, and to enforce these standards.
4. Significant public good results from the practice of the profession.

Many occupations require judgement everyday. A secretary must decide what work to tackle first. An auto mechanic must decide if a part is sufficiently worn to require complete replacement, or if rebuilding will do. In a profession, "judgement" refers to making significant decisions based on formal training and experience. In general, the decisions will have serious impact on people's lives and will often have important implications regarding the spending of large amounts of money.

Discretion can have two different meanings. The first definition involves being discrete in the performance of one's duties by keeping information about customers, clients, and patients confidential. This confidentiality is essential for a trusting relationship and is a hallmark of professions. While many jobs might involve some discretion, this definition implies a high level of significance to the information that must be kept private by a professional. The other definition of discretion involves the ability to make decisions autonomously. Many people are allowed to use their discretion in making choices while performing their jobs. However, the significance of the decision marks the difference between a job and a profession.

1.12.1 Who is a Professional—An Analysis

An athlete who is paid for her appearances is referred to as a *professional athlete*. Clearly, being a paid athlete does involve sophisticated skills that most people do not possess, and these skills are not capable of mechanization. However, substantial judgement and discretion are not called for on the part of athletes in their "professional" lives, so athletes fail the first part of the definition of "professional". Interestingly though, professional athletes are frequently viewed as role models and are often disciplined for a lack of discretion in their personal lives. Athletes require extensive training, not of a formal nature, but more of a practical nature acquired through practice and coaching. Thus, although they are highly trained and very well compensated, athletes are not professionals in the strict sense of the term.

Similarly, carpenters require special skills to perform their jobs, but many aspects of their work can be mechanized, and little judgement or discretion is required. Training in carpentry is not formal, but rather is practical by way of apprenticeships. No organizations or societies are required. However, carpentry certainly does meet an aspect of the public good—providing shelter is fundamental to society (the carpenter plays a major role in building homes), although perhaps not to the same extent as do professions such as medicine. Thus, carpentry also does not meet the basic requirements to be a profession.

1.12.2 Medicine and Law

Medicine certainly fits the definition of a profession given previously. It requires very sophisticated skills that can't be mechanized, it requires judgement as to appropriate treatment plans for individual patients, and it requires discretion. Although medicine requires extensive practical training learned through an apprenticeship called a residency, it also requires much formal training (four years of undergraduation (MBBS), three to four years of clinical experience (internship/house surgency), and extensive hands–on practice in patient care). In India, medicine has a special society (IMA) to which a large number of practicing physicians belong and participate. IMA plays a major role in the regulation of medical colleges, set standards for practice of the profession, and enforces codes of ethical behaviour for its members. Finally, healing the sick and helping to prevent disease clearly involve the public good. By the definition we have already given, medicine clearly qualifies as a profession.

Similarly, *law* is a profession. It involves sophisticated skills acquired through extensive formal training, and serves an important aspect of the public good. The difference between athletics and carpentry on one hand and law and medicine on the other is clear. The first two really cannot be considered professions, and the latter two most certainly are.

1.13 ENGINEERING AS A PROFESSION

Using medicine and law as examples of professions, it is now time to consider whether engineering is a profession. Certainly, engineering requires extensive and sophisticated skills. The essence of engineering design is judgement: how to use the available materials, component devices, etc. to reach specified objectives. Discretion is required in engineering: Engineers are required to keep their employers' or clients' intellectual property and business information confidential. Also, a primary concern of any engineer is the safety of the public that will use the products and devices he designs. There is always a trade-off between safety and other engineering issues in a design requiring discretion on the part of the engineer to ensure that the design serves its purpose and fills its market niche safely.

The point about mechanization needs to be addressed a little more carefully with respect to engineering. Certainly, once a design has been performed, it can easily be replicated without the interventions of an engineer. However, each new situation that demands a new design or a modification of an existing design requires an engineer. Industry commonly uses many computer-based tools for generating designs, such as computer-aided design (CAD) software. This should not be mistaken for mechanization of engineering. CAD is simply a tool used by engineers, not a replacement for the skills of an actual engineer.

Engineering requires extensive formal training. Four years of undergraduate training leading to a bachelor's degree in an engineering program is essential, followed by work under the supervision of an experienced engineer. Many engineering jobs even require advanced degrees beyond the bachelor's degree. The work of engineers serves the public good by providing communication systems, transportation, energy resources, and medical diagnostic and treatment equipment, to name only a few. Before passing final judgement on the professional status of engineering, the nature of engineering societies requires a little consideration. Each discipline within engineering has a professional society, such as the IEEE for electrical engineers and the ASME for mechanical engineers. These societies serve to set professional standards and frequently work with schools of engineering to set standards for admission and curricula. Unlike law and medicine, each specialty of engineering has its own society.

It is clear that engineering meets all the definitions of a profession. Also, engineering practice has much in common with medicine and law. Interestingly, although they are professionals, engineers do not yet hold the same status within society that physicians and reputed lawyers do.

1.14 PROFESSIONAL SOCIETIES

Sociologists who study the nature of professional societies describe two different models of professions, sometimes referred to as the social contract and the business models. The social-contract model views professional societies as being set up primarily to further the public good, as described in the definition of a profession already given. According to this model, there is an implicit social contract involved with professions. Society grants the professions perks such as high pay, a high status in society, and the ability to self-regulate. In return for these perks, society gets the services provided by the profession.

A perhaps more cynical view of professions is provided by the business model. According to this model, professions function as a means for furthering the economic advantage of the members. Put another way, professional organizations are labour unions for the elite, strictly limiting the number of practitioners of the profession, controlling the working conditions for professionals, and artificially inflating the salaries of its members. An analysis of both models in terms of law and medicine would show that there are ways in which these professions exhibit aspects of both of these models.

Where does engineering fit into the picture? Engineering is certainly a service-oriented profession and thus fits into the social contract model quite nicely. Although some engineers might wish to see engineering professional societies function more according to the business model, they currently do not function that way. The engineering societies have virtually no clout with major engineering employers to set wages and working conditions or to help engineers resolve ethical disputes with their employers.

1.15 CORE QUALITIES OF PROFESSIONAL PRACTITIONERS

Professional practitioners, of all disciplines, need six core qualities:

1. Integrity—openness and honesty, both with themselves and with others
2. Independence—to be free of secondary interests with other parties
3. Impartiality—to be free of bias and unbalanced interests
4. Responsibility—the recognition and acceptance of personal commitment
5. Competence—a thorough knowledge of the work they undertake to do
6. Discretion—care with communications, trustworthiness.

With growing specialization in the division of work, there is the danger of the 'expert' becoming focused purely on technical matters. It is important to note how this can affect the perception of the professional engineer, discouraging holistic thinking and inhibiting the full breadth of his work.

Integrity. This involves the discovery and communication of the truth. It is not simply truthfulness or avoid telling lies, but the capacity to communicate the truth in such a way as to enable the client and others to make informed decisions. Honesty and integrity are essential for the development of trust. It leads to consistency of character and operation in different situations and contexts. A good test of this is not just consistent operation in different contexts but also how the individual operates when there is nobody around, testing consistency and truth against personal attributes.

Independence. The professional is independent of pressure group. To be involved with either the employer or an action group in such a way that professional judgement is clouded is to lose professional autonomy. To achieve this independence, the professional must understand the situation and the key players in that situation. Independence enables the person not to be drawn into the concerns of any particular group. It presupposes the willingness and ability to take responsibility for decisions. By virtue of his special knowledge, the professional has an intrinsic authority. He also has an extrinsic authority vested in him by virtue of the position he holds. It is important to recognize that such authority leads many people to accept directions given by him despite any clearly unacceptable outcomes. Their personal responsibilities may be denied and transferred to the authority figure. Professionals must respect and encourage others to accept their own responsibilities.

Impartiality. Impartiality enables the professional to fulfill his contracts with his client, and to treat all parties equally. There is a need not to give primacy to self-interest, self-advancement, pressures of management roles, since in so doing, priorities for the achievement of programmes and cost targets may cloud professional judgements.

Responsibility. Responsibility involves the realistic assessment of skills and capacities and the acceptance of their possibilities and limitations. This is a core virtue on enabling the professional to acknowledge the responsibility of others, to accept personal responsibility and to work as a team—an essential part of modern engineering projects. Problems arise when professionals develop an inflated sense of responsibility, seeing themselves as responsible for more than they can be or ought to be. Realism is critical to ensure the best contribution from all members of the team.

Competence. Perseverance is necessary for the acquisition of technical competence and for its application in solving technical problems. This involves the capacity to strive for and maintain competence in professional practice. Competence is essential if the professional is to fulfill his or her responsibilities to society. The ethical requirement is in the acknowledgement of the need to be competent, rather than in the competence itself.

Discretion. In the course of projects, the professional will become aware of many aspects of the affairs of clients, contractors or other interested parties, and for him to retain the essential trust of those parties is important. Information must be treated on a 'need to know' basis, and not transmitted unnecessarily to others. In some cases, on defense projects, for example, consultants will be under an agreement not to divulge information to others. The responsibility placed upon the professional to act on behalf of others will be increased, his impartiality and independence assuming great importance. He must be able to raise matters of concern with his client and, if need be, with higher authorities if he is seriously concerned about the consequences of some action.

The engineer can be considered as playing several roles in society. He can be a

- Saviour — the engineer as the key player in the creation of a society with the development of technology and material prosperity for all.
- Guardian — ensuring the best interests of society, based upon engineering knowledge.
- Bureaucratic servant — a servant to managers, translating directives into achievements.

- Social servant — an obedient social servant to others.
- Game player — playing to political and economic game rules—playing successfully within the organization—competing to win.

In all of these roles, the engineer can act in different capacities; he can be a consultant, an employee, a manager, and an employer. These roles can frequently produce conflicts of interest.

1.16 PROFESSIONAL INSTITUTIONS

The profession as a whole has to be consistent and be able to relate values to practice. Without this, the recognition of the profession as a body of experts concerned for public welfare will be eroded, and with that will go whatever is essential to the functioning of any professional relationship. The existence of an institution of professionals is essential for the development and maintenance of professional virtues. It enables the individual professional to reflect upon his own integrity and to learn from the experience of others, transmitting the culture from generation to generation. It provides an external perspective which enables proper reflection and responsibility.

An institution can:

- Enable the professional development of moral awareness, skills, responsibility and identity, through codes, dialogues and training.
- Ensure that its processes and organization are conducive to the development of moral responsibility.
- Provide support and the opportunity for professionals to work through decision making and any conflict of interest.
- Regulate the practice of the individual professional.
- Play a major role in communicating with the public.
- Set standards for admissions to institutions and for initial and continuing professional training.
- Act as a learned society, contributing to the advancement of science and technology of engineering.

The professional institution must avoid the moral ambiguity of acting as a body protecting the interests of its individual members such as a trade union or trade association. It must be concerned with ensuring the highest standards of professional service to the community by regulating standards and criteria for membership. The institution should ensure sound practice by all its members.

1.17 OPERATING IN A PLURALISTIC SOCIETY

Working within a pluralistic society has several implications for business:

1. Business power is kept in balance by various groups such as the environmental group.

2. Business interest can be expressed by joining groups like the chamber of commerce.
3. Business participation in projects of other responsible groups for the purpose of bettering society.
4. In a pluralistic society there can be conflict or disagreement among groups.
5. In such a society, one group is quite aware of what other groups are doing.

1.18 ENVIRONMENTS AND THEIR IMPACT

It is sometimes thought that the economic environment is of interest only to businesses whose socially approved mission is the production and distribution of goods and services that people want and can pay for. But it is also of the greatest importance to other types of organized enterprises. A government agency takes resources usually from tax payers and provides services desired by the public. A church takes contributions from members and serves their religious and social needs. A university gets its resources through grants from government, fees from students, and through contributions made by private individuals or corporates and transforms these into educational and research services.

1.18.1 Economic Environment—Capital

Almost every kind of organization needs capital—machinery, buildings, inventories of goods, office equipment, tools of all kinds and cash. Some of these may be produced by the organization itself, as when a business builds its own machinery or a temple provides food for its devotees. Cash resources may also be generated within an organization to buy capital items outside, as when business profits are used to purchase equipment or when a university collects parking fees to pay for the building of parking structures. But organized enterprises are usually dependent for capital requirements on various suppliers whose job it is to produce materials and other items of capital that an organization requires for its operation.

1.18.2 Labour

Another important input from the economic environment is the availability, quality and price of labour. In some societies untrained common labour may be plentiful, while highly trained labour may be in short supply. Engineers may be scarce at one time and plentiful at another, as has occurred in the ups and downs of the defense and space operations.

1.18.3 Price Levels

The input side of an enterprise is clearly affected by the price level changes. If prices go up fairly rapidly, as happened in most part of the world in 1970s and early 1980s, the turbulence created in the environment on both the input and output sides can be severe. Inflation not only upsets businesses but also has highly disturbing influences on every kind of organization through its effect on the costs of labour, materials, and other items.

1.18.4 Government Fiscal and Tax Policies

Another important input to enterprise is the nature of government fiscal and tax policies. Although, these are, strictly speaking, aspects of the political environment, their economic impact on all enterprises is tremendous. Government control of the availability of credit through fiscal policy has considerable impact not only on business but also on most non-business operations. Similarly, Government tax policy affects every segment of the society. The way taxes are levied is also important not only to business but the people generally. For example, if taxes on business or profits are too high, the incentive to go into business or stay in it tends to drop, and investors will look elsewhere to invest their capital. If taxes are levied on sales, prices will rise and people will tend to buy less. If heavy taxes are placed in real estates, people may find it too expensive to own a house and may go to cheaper, less comfortable living quarters.

1.18.5 Customers

Without customers business cannot exist. But to capture customers, a business must try to find out what people want and will buy. To be sure, the expectations and demands of the various public served by organized enterprise are influenced by non-economic as well as economic factors in the environment. The principal ones are people's attitudes, desires and expectations, many of which arise from the cultural pattern prevalent in the social environment. Still, economic factors play a major role. People want as much benefit as possible for their money whether it goes to business, government or charitable institutions.

Another factor in the market is the appearance of substitute products. For example, publishers of magazines saw their market eroded when advertisers shifted to television. Also, people like different products. Some want a power boat, others want a sail boat, and still others do not want a boat at all. The needs of industrial buyers change as their products change, as new processes are developed and as different equipment and materials come on the market. In the long run, any enterprise has to serve the different and changing needs of customers. To do otherwise is a sure road to enterprise failure.

1.18.6 Technology

One of the most pervasive factors in the environment is technology. It is science that provides knowledge, and it is technology that uses it. The term **technology** refers to the sum total of the knowledge we have of ways to do things. It includes inventions, techniques and vast stores of organized knowledge about everything. But its main influence is on ways of doing things, on how we design, produce, distribute, and sell goods as well as services.

1.18.7 Impact of Technology: Benefits and Problems

The impact of technology is seen in new products, new machines, new tools, new materials and new services. A few of the benefits of technology are greater productivity, higher living standards, more leisure time, and a greater variety of products. Consider, for example, the great variety of cars available today subcompacts, compacts, intermediates, full sized automobiles, utility vehicles, and sports and speciality cars. Consider also the many body styles, the various colours, and the many options in engines (sizes), transmissions (manual, automatic) and brakes (mechanical, power). In addition, one may select tinted glass, power windows, power steering, automatic speed control, air conditioning, special mirrors, and vinyl roofs, a sun roof and various interior and exterior trims.

The benefits of technology must be weighed against the problems associated with technological developments such as traffic jam, polluted air and water, energy shortages, and loss of privacy through the application of computer technology. What is needed is a balanced approach that takes advantage of technology and at the same time minimizes some of the undesirable side effects.

1.18.8 Categories and Technological Change

1. Increased ability to master time and distance for the movement of freight and passengers: rail roads, automobiles, trucks, air planes, space vehicles (to some extent).
2. Increased ability to generate, store, transport and distribute energy: electricity, nuclear power, and laser.
3. Increased ability to design new materials and change the properties of others so that they serve the needs better: steel alloys, synthetic fibres, plastics, and new drugs.
4. Mechanization or automation of physical processes: the large number of labour saving devices from Hargreaves's spinning jenny in 1770 to the largely automatic subway systems in San Francisco and Washington.
5. Mechanization or automation of certain processes: the computer which greatly expands our ability to store, manipulate, select and supply data.
6. Extension of the human ability to sense things: radar, the electron microscope, and night vision instruments.
7. Increased understanding of individual and group behaviour and how to deal with it: psychological bases of motivation, group behaviour patterns, and improved management techniques.

8. Increased understanding of diseases and their treatment: vaccination for polio, kidney transplants, antibiotic treatment of infections.

1.18.9 Social Environment

The social environment is made up of the attitudes, desires, expectations, degrees of intelligence and education, beliefs, and customs of people in a given group or society. The political and legal environment, is primarily that complex of laws, regulations and government agencies and their actions which affect all kinds of enterprises, often to varying degrees. The concept of social responsibilities requires organizations to consider the impact of their actions on society. The ethical environment, which could well be included as an element in the social environment, includes sets of generally accepted and practiced standards of personal conduct. These standards may or may not be codified by law, but for any group to which they are meant to apply, they often acquire the force of law.

1.19 COMPLEXITY OF ENVIRONMENTAL FORCES

The interweaving of these environmental elements makes their study and comprehension exceptionally difficult. Social desires, expectations and pressures give rise to laws and standards of ethics. Social forces, including ethics normally arise before laws are passed since the legislative process is notably reactive in the sense that it acts when a crisis is at hand but seldom before.

1.19.1 Political Environment

The attitudes and actions of political and government leaders and legislators do change with the ebb and flow of social demands and beliefs. Many legislators who strongly supported involvement in Vietnam did a complete turnabout when people became disenchanted with the outcome of the war. In many communities, strong sentiments about air and water pollution control subsided when plants that were unable to meet new standards had to be shut down. Government affects virtually every enterprise and every aspect of life. It promotes business by stimulating economic expansion and development by providing financial assistance. Finally, government is also the biggest customer, purchasing goods and services.

1.19.2 Legal Environment

Every manager is encircled by a web of laws, regulations, and court decisions, not only on the national level but also on the state and local levels. Some are designed to protect workers, consumers, and communities. Others are designed to make contracts enforceable and to protect property rights. Many are designed to regulate the behaviour of managers and their subordinates in business and other enterprises. There is relatively little that a manger can do in any organization that is not in some way concerned with and often specifically controlled by a law or regulation. Managers are expected to know the legal restrictions and requirements applicable to their actions. Thus, it is understandable that managers, especially in business and government, usually have a legal expert close at hand as they make their decisions.

1.20 SOCIAL ATTITUDES, BELIEFS, AND VALUES

Managers of various enterprises have been criticised for not being responsive to the social attitudes, beliefs, and values of particular individuals, groups or societies. But attitudes and values differ among workers and employers, rich and poor people, college students and alumni, accountants and engineers. This variety makes it difficult for managers to design an environment conducive to performance and satisfaction. It is even more difficult to respond to these forces when they are outside the enterprise.

1.20.1 Social Responsibility and Social Responsiveness

A concept that is newer but still very similar to social responsibility is social responsiveness which in simple terms means "the ability of a corporation to relate its operations and policies to the social environment in ways that are mutually beneficial to the company and to the society". Both the definitions focus on corporations, but these concepts should be expanded to include enterprises other than businesses, and to encompass relationships within an enterprise. The main difference between social responsibility and social responsiveness is that the latter implies actions and the "how" of enterprise responses.

1.20.2 Arguments for Social Involvement of Business

1. Public needs have changed leading to changed expectations. Business received its charter from society and has to respond to the needs of society.
2. The creation of a better social environment benefits both society and business. Society gains through better neighbourhoods and employment opportunities, and business benefits from a better community since the community is the source of its workforce and the consumer of its products and services.
3. Social involvement discourages additional government regulation and intervention. The result is greater freedom and more flexibility in decision making for business.
4. Business has a great deal of power and should be accompanied by an equal amount of responsibility.
5. Modern society is an interdependent system and the internal activities of the enterprise have an impact on the external environment.

6. Social involvement may be in the interest of stock holders.
7. Problems can become profits. Items that may once have been considered waste (for example empty soft drinks cans) can be profitably used again.
8. Social involvement creates a favourable pubic image. Thus a firm may attract customers, employees and investors.
9. Business should try to solve the problems that other institutions have not been able to solve. After all, business has a history of coming up with novel ideas.
10. Business has the resources. Specifically, business should use its talented managers and specialists, as well as its capital resources, to solve some of society's problems.
11. It is better to prevent social problems through business involvement than to cure them. It may be easier to address the grievances of the disgrunted employees and the unemployed than to cope with social unrest.

1.20.3 Arguments against Social Involvement of Business

1. The primary task of business is to maximize profit by focusing strictly on economic activities. Social involvement could reduce economic efficiency.
2. In the final analysis, society must pay for the social involvement of business through higher prices. Social involvement would create excessive cost for business which cannot commit its resources to social action.
3. Social involvement can create a weakened international balance of payments situation. The cost of social programmes would have to be added to the price of the product.
4. Business has enough power, and additional social involvement would further increase its power and influence.
5. Business people lack the social skills to deal with the problems of society. Their training and experience with the economic matters and their skills may not be pertinent to social problems.
6. There is a lack of accountability of business to society. Unless accountability can be established, business should not get involved.
7. There is no complete support for involvement in social actions. Consequently, disagreements among groups with different view points will cause friction.

1.20.4 Social Audit

The social audit has been defined as "a commitment to systematic assessment of and reporting on some meaningful, definable domain of the company's activities that have social impact". One may distinguish between two types of audits. The first is required by the government and involves, for example, pollution control, product performance requirements, and equal employment standards. The second kind of social audit concerns a great variety of voluntary social programmes.

1.20.5 Institutionalizing Ethics

Managers, especially top managers, do have a responsibility to create an organizational environment that fosters ethical decision making by institutionalizing ethics. This means applying ethical concepts in daily action. This can be accomplished in three ways: (i) by establishing an appropriate company policy or a code of ethics; (ii) by using a formally appointed ethics committee; and (iii) by teaching ethics in management development programmes.

1.21 CODE OF ETHICS

Morality refers to those standards of conduct that apply to all individuals within society rather than only to members of a special group. These are the standards that every rational person wants every other person to follow and include standards such as the following:

- Respect the rights of others
- Show fairness in your dealings with others
- Be honest in all actions
- Keep promises and contracts
- Consider the welfare of others
- Show compassion to others

By professional ethics we mean those standards of conduct that every member of a profession expects every other member to follow. These ethical standards apply to members of that group. Like morality, standards of ethical conduct are value based. Some values that are pertinent to professional ethics include:

- Honesty and truth
- Honour—showing respect, integrity and reputation for achievement
- Knowledge—gained through education and experience
- Efficiency—producing efficiently with minimum of effort
- Diligence—persistent effort
- Loyalty—allegiance to employer's goals
- Confidentiality—dependable in safeguarding information
- Protecting public safety and health

Note that some of these values are directed towards the employer (e.g. diligence), some towards the customer (e.g. confidentiality), some towards the profession (e.g. honour), and some towards society (e.g. public health and safety.) These values reflect the professional's value obligations (refer to Appendices 1 and 2).

1.21.1 Purpose of Code of Ethics

Primarily, a code of ethics provides a framework for ethical judgement for a professional. No code can be totally comprehensive and cover all possible ethical situations that a professional engineer is likely to encounter. Rather, codes serve as a starting point for ethical decision making. A code can also express the commitment to ethical conduct shared by members of a profession. It is important to note that ethical codes do not establish new ethical principles. They simply reiterate principles and standards that are already accepted as responsible engineering practice. A code expresses these principles in a coherent, comprehensive, and acceptable manner. Finally, a code defines the roles and responsibilities of professionals. A code of ethics is never a substitute for sound judgement. A code of ethics is not a legal document. One cannot be arrested for violating its provisions although expulsion from the professional society might result from code violations.

How does a code of ethics achieve these goals? First, a code of ethics helps create an environment within a profession where ethical behaviour is the norm. It also serves as a guide or reminder of how to act in specific situations. A code of ethics can also be used to boost an individual who is being pressured by a superior to behave unethically. A code of ethics can also strengthen the individual's position by indicating that there is a collective sense of correct behaviour; there is strength in numbers. Finally, a code of ethics can indicate to others that the profession is seriously concerned about responsible, professional conduct. A code of ethics, however, should not be used as "window dressing"—an attempt by an organization to appear to be committed to ethical behaviour when it really is not.

1.21.2 Objections to Codes

First, relatively few practising engineers are members of professional societies and so do not necessarily feel compelled to abide by their codes. Many engineers who are members of professional societies are not aware of the existence of the society's code, or if they are aware of it, they have never read it. Even among engineers who know about their society's code, consultation of the code is rare. There are also objections that the engineering codes often have internal conflicts, but do not give a method for resolving the conflict. Finally, codes can be coercive: They foster ethical behaviour with a stick rather than with a carrot. Despite these objections, codes are in widespread use today and are generally thought to serve a useful function.

1.21.3 Codes of Engineering Societies

Early in the current century, these codes were mostly concerned with issues of how to conduct business. For example, many early codes had clauses forbidding advertising of services or prohibiting competitive bidding by engineers for design projects. Codes also spelled out the duties that engineers had toward their employers. Relatively less emphasis than today was given to issues of service to the public and safety. This imbalance changed greatly in recent decades as public perceptions and concerns about the safety of engineered products and devices have changed. Now, most codes emphasize commitments to safety, public health, and even environmental protection as the most important duties of the engineer.

1.21.4 Resolving Internal Conflicts in Codes

One of the objections to code of ethics is the internal conflicts that can exist within them, with no instructions on how to resolve these conflicts. An example of this problem would be a situation in which an employer asks or even orders an engineer to implement a design that the engineer feels will be unsafe. How can this conflict be resolved? There is no implication in this or any other code that all clauses are equally important. Rather, there is a hierarchy within the code. Some clauses take precedence over others although there is generally no explicit indication in the code of what the hierarchy is. The dilemma presented above is easily resolved within the context of this hierarchy. The duty to protect the safety of the public is paramount and takes precedence over the duty to the employer. In this case, the code provides very clear support to the engineer who must convince his supervisor that he can not design the product as requested. Unfortunately, not all internal conflicts in codes of ethics are so easily resolved.

1.21.5 Other Types of Codes of Ethics

Professional societies are not the only organizations that codified their ethical standards. Many other organizations have also developed codes of ethics for various purposes similar to those of the professional engineering organizations. For example, codes for the ethical use of computers have been developed, and student organizations in universities have framed student codes of ethics. Even if the professional codes were widely adopted and recognized by practicing engineers, there would still be some value to the corporate codes since a corporation can tailor its code to the individual circumstances and unique mission of the company. As such, these codes tend to be relatively long and detailed, incorporating many rules specific to the practices of the company. For example, corporate codes frequently spell out in detail the company policies on business practices, relationships with suppliers, relationships with government agencies, compliance with government regulations, health and safety issues, issues related to environmental protection, equal employment opportunity and affirmative action, sexual harassment, and diversity and racial/ethnic tolerance. Since corporate codes are coercive in nature your continued employment by the company depends on your compliance with the company code. These codes tend to be longer and more detailed in order to provide very clear and specific guidelines to the employees.

1.22 SOLVING ETHICAL CONFLICTS

It is probably safe to say that every engineer must resolve at least one ethical dilemma over the duration of his or her career. If the engineer mishandles the situation, his or her career can be damaged even in cases where he or she is trying to do the right thing. Therefore, it is important to know how to handle ethical conflicts and to have thought about conflict resolution before being confronted by a problem. A difficult problem for engineers arises from the dual obligation to serve diligently and with loyalty to both their employer and society. The vast majority of businesses aim to be honest and responsible corporate citizen, but the conflict between profit and societal good is potentially always present.

1.22.1 Guidelines

Ethical decision making is not easy. However, the chances for successfully resolving ethical conflict can be greatly increased by following a systematic procedure. One set of guidelines that will help ensure meeting one's professional responsibilities is given below. Except under the unusual circumstances of imminent danger to the public, it is important that all internal steps be explored before seeking options outside the organization. The process of seeking resolution to an ethical conflict within the organization is usually handled through an appeals process within management or by the complaint process through the office of the ombudsman or the ethics officer. Seeking resolution outside the organization is usually called whistle blowing. A step-by-step procedure for resolving an ethical conflict through an internal and external appeal process is given in the succeeding section.

1.22.2 Procedure for Solving Ethical Conflicts

1. Internal Appeal Option

A Individual preparation

- Maintain a record of the event and details
- Examining the company's internal appeals process
- Be familiar with the laws that could protect you
- Identify alternative courses of action
- Decide on the outcome that you want the appeal to accomplish

B Communicate with your immediate supervisor

- Initiate informal discussion
- Make a formal written appeal
- Indicate your intention of starting internal process of appeal

C Initiate appeal through the internal chain of command

- Maintain formal contacts as to where the appeal stands
- Inform your intention to pursue an external solution

2. External Appeal Option

A Individual actions

- Engage legal counsel
- Contact your professional society

B Contact your client (if applicable)

C Contact the media

The steps that the individual should take in preparation for disclosure of unethical behaviour are straightforward. Once you have studied and documented the facts and formulated a plan for appeal, you should discuss the matter with your immediate supervisor. Failure to fully communicate your concerns to your immediate supervisor or secretly going over his or her head to higher levels is viewed as disloyalty and will be viewed negatively by all involved, even your supervisor's superior. However, if after fully discussing the issue with your supervisor you feel that your supervisor is not willing or able to take appropriate action, then inform your supervisor in writing of your intention to appeal beyond that level.

The process of appealing an ethical conflict within the company is usually similar to the process of interacting with your immediate supervisor on the issue. You should have the facts and a plan of how you would like to see the issue resolved. Formal steps should follow informal discussions, and steps within the appeal chain should not be bypassed. If the internal appeal does not resolve the ethical conflict, then you should notify the company that you intend to continue with an external review of the problem.

Before expressing any public concern, legal advice should be obtained. A lawyer can identify the desired course of action and legal pitfalls in your external appeal. However, while lawyers understand the legal issues, they may not have the technical background to evaluate the technical adequacy of your arguments. For this reason, it might be helpful to involve an engineering professional society as an impartial judge of your arguments. Engineering societies vary widely in their willingness to become involved in this kind of activities.

If your company worked for a client in the issue about which you are concerned, then the client should be approached before going public. The client may pressure your company to resolve the issue internally or he may provide the resources to obtain an unbiased review of the issue. The last resort is public disclosure by contacting the press and the TV news channels. This is often called *whistle blowing*.

1.23 ETHICAL JUDGEMENT

Engineers mostly work in the business world and they are therefore required to perform their duties within the laws of the nation. But more than this, engineering is the profession that is critical to the advancement of society.

How engineers do their jobs determines what kind of world future generations will enjoy. Thus, the practice of engineering without question will involve you in making ethical judgements.

1.23.1 Law

The law is a formalized code of conduct describing what society feels is the proper way to behave. Statutory law is created by a federal or state legislative body. Case law arises from the decisions of the courts. Ethical conduct is the behaviour that is described by society and is separate from the minimum standards of the law.

1.23.2 Contract

Engineers should be familiar with contracts and liability and especially product liability. A contract is an agreement between two parties to do or not to do something. It consists of an offer, an acceptance of the offer and a consideration, the exchange of something of value. A contract is discharged when agreement has been performed to the satisfaction of both the parties. A breach of contract occurs when one party fails to perform that part of the contract.

1.23.3 Liability

Liability means being bound or obligated to pay damages or restitution. Two common ways of incurring liability are breaching a contract or committing a tort. A tort is a civil wrong committed against a person or the business, property, or reputation that causes damage. Common examples of torts are fraud, misrepresentation, negligence, and product liability.

1.23.4 Product Liability

Product liability is the legal action by which an injured party seeks to recover damages for personal injury or property loss from the producer or seller of a product. A law under which product liability is tried has evolved to a standard of strict product liability. Under this theory of law, the plaintiff must prove that:

1. The product was defective and dangerous.
2. The defect existed at the time the product left the dependent's control.
3. The defect caused the harm.
4. The harm is appropriately assignable to the identified defect. According to earlier laws, manufacturers were liable only when they could be proved negligent or unreasonably careless, now the situation is different.

While the boundary between legal and illegal acts is generally well defined by the law, the distinction between what is ethical and what is unethical is much less well defined.

Chapter 2

Moral Reasoning and Ethical Theories

Moral reasons require us to respect other people as well as ourselves, to care for others' good as well as our own. Moral reasons, for instance, involve respecting persons by being fair and just with them, respecting their rights, keeping promises, avoiding unnecessary offence and pain to them, and not resorting to cheating or practising dishonesty. They also concern with caring for others by being sometimes willing to help them (especially when they are in distress), showing gratitude for favours, and empathizing with their suffering. Furthermore, these are concerns that reach beyond personal interactions or the minimal requirements of workaday moral duty, such as encouraging engineers and others to seek work where they can contribute to, say, wiser uses of the world's depletable resources.

2.1 THEORIES OF RIGHT ACTION

There are four ethical theories that will be considered here, each differing according to what is held to be the most important moral concept:

1. *Utilitarianism* seeks to produce the most utility, defined as a balance between good and bad consequences of an action, taking into account the consequences for everyone affected.
2. *Duty ethics* contends that there are duties that should be performed (the duty to treat others fairly or the duty not to injure others) regardless of whether these acts lead to the most good.
3. *Rights ethics* emphasizes that we all have moral rights, and any action that violates these rights is ethically unacceptable. Like duty ethics, the ultimate overall good of the actions is not taken into account.
4. *Virtue ethics* regards those actions as right that manifest good traits (virtues), and regards those actions as bad that display bad traits (vices). This ethical theory focuses on the type of person we should strive to be. These theories are now briefly discussed.

2.1.1 Utilitarianism

Utilitarianism holds that those actions are good that serve to maximize human well-being. The emphasis in utilitarianism is not on maximizing the well-being of the individual, but rather on maximizing the well-being of society as a whole, and as such it is somewhat of a collectivist approach. An example of this theory is the building of dams. Dams often lead to great benefit to society by providing stable supplies of drinking water, flood control, and recreational opportunities. However, these benefits often come at the expense of people who live in areas that will be flooded by the dam and are required to find new homes. Utilitarianism tries to balance the needs of society with the needs of the individual, with an emphasis on what will provide the most benefit to most people.

Utilitarianism is fundamental to many types of engineering analysis, including risk-benefit analysis and cost-benefit analysis. However, as good as the utilitarian principle sounds, there are some problems associated with it. First, as seen in the example of the building of a dam, sometimes what is best for everyone may be bad for a particular individual or group of individuals. Another objection to utilitarianism is that its implementation depends greatly on knowing what will lead to the maximum good. Frequently, it is impossible to know exactly what the consequences of an action are. It is often impossible to do a complete set of experiments to determine all of the potential outcomes, especially when humans are involved as subjects of the experiments. So, maximizing the benefit to society involves guesswork and the risk that the best guess might be wrong. Despite these objections, utilitarianism is a very valuable tool for ethical problem solving, providing one way of looking at engineering ethics cases.

Act utilitarianism focuses on individual actions rather than on rules. The best known proponent of act utilitarianism was John Stuart Mill (1806–1873), who felt that most of the common rules of morality (don't steal, be honest, don't harm others) are good guidelines derived from centuries of human experience. However, Mill felt that individual actions should be judged based on whether the most good was produced in a given situation, and rules should be broken if doing so will lead to the most good. *Rule utilitarianism* differs from act utilitarianism as it holds that moral rules are most important. Rule utilitarians contend that, although adhering to these rules might not always maximize good in a particular situation, overall, adhering to moral rules will ultimately lead to the most good. These two different types of utilitarianism can lead to slightly different results when applied to specific situations.

2.1.2 Cost-Benefit Analysis

Fundamentally, this type of analysis is just an application of utilitarianism. In cost-benefit analysis, the costs of project are assessed, as are the benefits.

Only those projects with the highest ratio of benefits to costs will be implemented. This principle is similar to the utilitarian goal of maximizing the overall good. As with utilitarianism, there are pitfalls in the use of cost-benefit analysis. While it is often easy to predict the costs for most projects, the benefits that are derived from them are often harder to predict and to assign a monetary value to. For example, from a pure cost-benefit discussion, it might seem that the building of a dam is an excellent idea. But this analysis will not include other issues such as whether the benefits outweigh the loss of a scenic wilderness area or the loss of an endangered species with no current economic value. Finally, it is also important to determine whether those who stand to reap the benefits are also those who will pay the costs. It is unfair to place all of the costs on one group while another reaps the benefits.

2.1.3 Duty Ethics and Right Ethics

These theories hold that those actions are good that respect the rights of the individual. A major proponent of duty ethics was Immanuel Kant (1724–1804) who held that moral duties are fundamental. Ethical actions are those actions that could be written down as a list of duties: be honest, do not cause suffering to other people, be fair to others, etc. These actions are our duties because they express respect for persons, have an unqualified regard for autonomous moral agents, and are universal principles. Once a person's duties are recognized , the ethically correct moral actions are obvious. In this formulation, ethical acts are a result of proper performance of one's duties.

Rights ethics was largely formulated by John Locke (1632–1704). It holds that people have fundamental rights that other people have a duty to respect. Duty ethics and rights ethics are just two sides of the same coin. Both these theories achieve the same end: Individual persons must be respected, and actions are ethical that maintain this respect for the individual. In duty ethics, people have duties, an important one of which is to protect the rights of others. And in rights ethics, people have fundamental rights that others have duties to protect.

There are problems with the duty and rights ethics theories that must be considered. First, the basic rights of one person (or group) may conflict with the basic rights of another group. Using the already cited example of the building of a dam, people have the right to use their property. If their land happens to be in the way of a proposed dam, then rights ethics would hold that this property right is paramount and is sufficient to stop the dam project. A single property holder's objection would require that the project be terminated. However, there is a need for others living in nearby communities to have a reliable water supply and to be safe from continual flooding. Who's rights are paramount here? Rights and duty ethics do not resolve this conflict very well; hence, the utilitarian approach of trying to determine the most good is more useful there. The second problem with duty and rights ethics is that these theories do not always account for the overall good of society very well. Since the emphasis is on the individual, the good of a single individual can be paramount compared to what is good for society as a whole. Rights ethics would come down clearly on the side of the individuals living along the route despite the overall advantage to society.

2.1.4 Which Theory to Use?

The good news is that in solving ethical problems, we do not have to choose from among these theories. Rather, we can use all of them to analyze a problem from different angles and see what result each of the theories gives us. This allows us to examine a problem from different perspectives to see what conclusion each one reaches. Frequently, the result will be the same even though the theories are very different.

Take, for example, a chemical plant near a small city that discharges a hazardous waste into the groundwater. If the city takes its water from wells, the water supply for the city will be compromised and significant health problems for the community may result. Rights ethics indicates that this pollution is unethical since it causes harm to many of the residents. A utilitarian analysis would probably also come to the same conclusion since the economic benefits of the plant would almost certainly be outweighed by the negative effects of the pollution and the costs required to ensure a safe municipal water supply. Virtue ethics would say that discharging wastes into groundwater is irresponsible and harmful to individuals and so should not be done. In this case, all the ethical theories lead to the same conclusion.

2.1.5 Uses of Ethical Theories

Ethical theories have three important uses: in understanding moral dilemmas, in justifying professional obligations and ideals, and in relating ordinary and professional morality.

Resolving moral dilemmas

1. Ethical theories aid in identifying the moral consideration or reasons that constitute a dilemma. Thus, virtue ethics construes the moral dilemma in terms of competing ideals of character and relationships, loyalty to employers and colleagues versus loyalty to the public. Utilitarianism construes the dilemma in terms of competing goods, and the safety of the public. Duty ethics indicates the duties to protect the public affected by the work and to respect his employer's legitimate authority to make management-level decisions about expenditures. And rights ethics emphasizes the rights of the public to be protected (or at least warned of dangers) and the rights of management to have their decisions respected.

2. Ethical theories provide more precise sense of what kinds of information are relevant to solving moral dilemma. All the theories agree that facts about the potential harm to the public are directly and urgently relevant.
3. The theories offer ways to rank the relevant moral considerations in order of importance, and thereby provide at least guidance in solving moral problems:
   (i) the special importance of right to life and to informed consent concerning risks to one's life;
   (ii) the importance of duties to protect the vulnerable public;
   (iii) the degree of immorality involved in death and risk of death compared to economic benefits to corporations.
4. The theories help us identify the full moral ramifications of alternative courses of action, urging a wide perspective on the moral implications of the options, and providing a systematic framework for comparing the alternatives.
5. The theories augment the precision with which we use moral terms, and provide frameworks for moral reasoning when discussing moral issues with colleagues.
6. By providing frameworks for development of moral arguments, the theories strengthen our ability to reach balanced and insightful judgements.

Justifying moral obligations. Ethical theories can be used to justify the general obligations of engineers and others involved in technological development.

Relating professional and ordinary morality. The special obligations concerning safety that engineers acquire as a consequence of their work are intimately connected with ordinary or everyday morality. The same ethical theories that are useful in expressing everyday moral experience are also useful in justifying the obligations of professionals.

To underscore this fact, consider four other views concerning the origin and justification of the safety (and other) obligations of engineers.

1. The engineers acquire moral obligations concerning safety by being subject to laws or enforced codes that require them to be so obligated. This constitutes a legalistic approach to morality, that is an attempt to model morality on the law or reduce it to legal para-legal considerations.
2. The engineers acquire special obligations by joining a professional society and thereby agree to live by that society's code of ethics. This view differs greatly from the first by emphasizing the voluntary act of agreeing to abide by a code rather than passively being subject to enforced laws and codes. Thus, it ties directly into our ordinary understanding of how promises and other self-committing acts generate obligations.

3. The engineers acquire safety obligations through contractual agreements by which they are hired by their companies or employers. An engineer who is hired as a safety inspector surely does acquire special work responsibility related to safety. And those responsibilities cannot be reduced merely to prudential concerns, that is, reduced to the attitude, such that not meeting them would lead to the loss of one's job or a promotion. Rather, they entail specific commitments to fulfill such job-related duties, and this means moral obligations have been generated.
4. The engineers tacitly promise the public to protect and safeguard them in the course of performing their tasks. In return, the public has largely underwritten engineering education through financial support for engineering colleges, and implicitly granted the profession as a whole certain privileges.

2.2 VARIETY OF MORAL ISSUES

Engineering disasters draw our attention and caution us about compromising safety beyond the level of acceptable risk. Examples: Challenger explosion, the accidents at the nuclear plants at Chernobyl and Three Mile Island and the chemical plant at Bhopal, the Exxon Valdez oil spill, natural disasters earthquakes in Gujarat, Iran, and indiscriminate uses of asbestos.

A related distinction contrasts two approaches to engineering ethics. One emphasizes typical, everyday problems that can take on significant proportions in an engineer's life or an entire engineering office (micro-ethics), the other addresses societal problems that are often ignored and are not addressed until they unexpectedly resurface on a regional or national scale (macro-ethics). Neither approach covers the entire spectrum of ethical problems engineers might encounter. Ongoing attention is needed to understand how one may affect the other in an engineer's professional and personal life.

2.3 MAJOR ETHICAL ISSUES

The decision to report to higher authorities demands careful judgement about the nature of the moral problems involved and about the consequences of such a decision. The following cases illustrate some of the difficulties an engineer may face:

- A junior engineer on a building site was given the task of developing plans, which should be checked by a senior. It soon became apparent that the plans were not being checked but simply stamped and sent on for work. He mentioned this to his immediate superior who dismissed the protest, asking how he thought they were to get any building done if they followed all the rules to the letter. Where should he go from here?

- A civil engineer frequently walked past a building site for which he had no responsibility and over time noted several problems with safety and with the quality of work. What should he do?
- A senior consultant engineer who had followed the correct procedures in the development of a major city centre building had it pointed out to him by one of the undergraduates with whom he worked in a university link, that there were serious design faults in the foundation of the building. What should he do?

These few cases demonstrate some of the critical issues involved. The need to report may involve criticism of the actions of colleagues of an organization, or even of oneself. Whose responsibility is it to report in these situations? Should it only be the professional who is directly involved? Are there any alternatives to such reporting? What will the effects be on the professional, his family and career, on the organization, etc? If it is right to report in this way, to whom should the professional report–to his professional body, to a government or other official body, to the senior management in his company, to concerned pressure groups, or to the press?

The principal features of such unusual reporting are as follows:

- The information is conveyed outside approved organizational channels, or in situations where the person conveying it is under pressure from supervisors or others not to report it.
- The information is new to, or is not fully known by, the person or group to whom it is being sent.
- The information is believed to represent a significant moral problem concerning the organization. Examples of such significant problems would be: criminal behaviour; unethical practices; injustices to workers within the organization; threats to public safety; breaches of local customs.

The method of reporting may depend upon the potential effects of the action on the organization, the professional, the public, and any other relevant body. Reporting requires a moral decision, an estimate of the extent of the problem, the nature of the professional responsibility, and the probable consequences of the various options. The reporter must be prepared to give way if his judgement is shown to be incorrect.

2.4 ANALYSIS OF ISSUE IN ETHICAL PROBLEMS

A first step in solving any ethical problem is to completely understand all of the issues involved. Once these issues are determined, frequently a solution to the problem becomes apparent. The issues involved in understanding ethical problems can be split into three categories: factual, conceptual, and moral.

Understanding these issues helps to put an ethical problem in the proper framework and often enables one to find out a solution.

2.5 THREE TYPES OF INQUIRY

Engineering ethics combines inquiries into values, meanings, and facts. Normative inquiries, which are most central, seek to identify the values that should guide individuals and groups. Conceptual inquiries seek to clarify important concepts or ideas, whether the ideas are expressed by single words or by statements and questions. Factual, descriptive inquiries seek to provide facts needed for understanding and resolving value issues.

2.5.1 Normative Inquiries

First, and foremost, engineering ethics involves normative inquiries aimed at identifying and justifying the morally desirable norms or standards that ought to guide individuals or groups. Normative questions are about what ought to be and what is good (bearing in mind that here our concern is with moral values). Some examples of normative questions:

How far does the obligation of engineers to protect public safety extend in given situations? When, if ever, should engineers be expected to blow the whistle on dangerous practices of the employers for whom they work? Whose values ought to be primary in making judgements about acceptable risks in a design for a public transport system: those of management, senior engineers, government, voters, or some combination of these? Which particular laws and organizational procedure affecting engineering practice are morally warranted? What moral rights should engineers be recognized as having in order to help them fulfill their professional obligations?

Intertwined with these practical questions, normative inquiries also have the theoretical goal of justifying particular moral judgements. For example, what are the reasons engineers have obligations to their employers, their clients, and the general public? How can professional ideals be justified in terms of more fundamental moral ideals? When and why is government justified in interfering with a free enterprise?

2.5.2 Conceptual Inquiries

Second, conceptual inquiries are directed toward clarifying the meaning of concepts, principles, and issues in engineering ethics. For example, what does "safety" mean and how is it related to the idea of "risk"? What does it mean when codes of ethics say engineers should "protect the safety, health, and welfare of the public"? What is a bribe? What is a profession and what defines professionals? Where moral concepts are of issue, normative and conceptual issues are tightly interwoven. Conceptual issues have to do with the meaning or applicability of an idea. In engineering ethics, this might mean defining what constitutes a bribe as opposed to an acceptable gift, or determining whether certain business information is proprietary. In the case of bribe, the value of the gift is probably a well-known fact. What is not known is whether accepting it will lead to unfair influence on a business decision. For example, conceptually it must be determined if the gift of tickets to a sporting event by a potential supplier of parts for your project is meant to influence your decision or is just a nice gesture between friends. Of course, like factual issues, conceptual issues are not always clear-cut and will often result in controversy.

Once the factual and conceptual issues have been resolved, at least to the extent possible, all that remains is to determine which moral principle is applicable to the situation. Resolution of moral issues is often more obvious. Once the problem is defined, it is usually clear which moral concept applies and the correct decision becomes obvious. In our example of a "gift" offered by a sales representative, once it is determined whether it is simply a gift or is really a bribe, then the appropriate action is obvious. If we determine that it is indeed a bribe, then it cannot ethically be accepted.

2.5.3 Factual Inquiries

Third, factual inquiries—also called descriptive inquiries—seek to uncover information bearing upon value issues. Where possible, researchers attempt to conduct factual inquiries using proven scientific techniques. They provide important information about the business realities of contemporary engineering profession, the effectiveness of professional societies in fostering moral conduct, the procedures used in making risk assessments, and psychological profiles of engineers. Determining the facts in these areas provides an understanding of the background conditions that generate moral problems. It also enables us to deal realistically with alternative ways of resolving those problems. Factual inquiries involve what is actually known about a case, i.e., what the facts are. Although this concept seems straightforward, the facts of a particular case are not always clear and may be controversial. An example of facts that are not necessarily clear can be found in the controversy in contemporary society regarding abortion rights. There is great disagreement over the point at which life begins and at which point a fetus can be legally protected.

In engineering, there are controversies over facts as well. For example, global warming is of great concern to society as we continue to emit greenhouse gases into the atmosphere. Greenhouse gases, such as carbon dioxide, trap heat in the atmosphere. This is thought to lead to a generalized warming of the atmosphere as emissions from automobiles and industrial plants increase the carbon dioxide concentration in the atmosphere. This issue is of great importance to engineers since they might be required to design new products or redesign old ones to comply with stricter environmental standards, if this warming effect indeed proves to be a problem. However, the global warming process is only barely understood and the need to curtail emission of these gases is a controversial topic. If it were known exactly what the effects of emitting greenhouse gases into the atmosphere would be, the engineer's role in reducing this problem would be clearer.

2.6 ENGINEERING AND MANAGEMENT DECISION

There are two separate areas of decision, engineering and management. The engineering decision is dominated by technical matters and by ethical concerns for safety. The management decision is different, focusing on responsibilities to the work force, the shareholders, the local community, the customer, and thus upon economic, legal and public image matters. Apart from those frequent situations where the roles of manager and engineer coincide, the engineer cannot avoid his responsibilities by delegating them to a manager. All major projects involve teamwork, and collective responsibility is more often the case than individual responsibility. His particular expertise may place the engineer in a better position to understand the risks involved. In such a case, he has a duty to inform his colleagues that the risk or hazard exists, and should his colleagues ignore such advice, then he has a clear duty to report the facts to some other effective authority.

A checklist of actions which the engineer should consider if he thinks there is a problem and that external reporting is called for, might include the following.

- Confirming that the risk to the public or to fellow workers warrants some action. This requires a careful sifting of the evidence to assess if the harm to the public is significant.
- Motives, personal and corporate, should be carefully examined at an early stage. A colleague may be able to help in the assessment of the decision-making process. The dangers to be avoided are either the heroic motive, with the engineer seeing himself as fighting a battle or the revenge motive.
- The evidence should be verified and well documented, with records kept. Once more this may mean consulting with other colleagues in gathering or analysing data.
- Determining the area of concern and identifying the appropriate referral agency. Establishing which agencies may have the authority to enforce rules and laws related to health and safety, race relations, etc. At this point the professional body might be asked to help clarify the issues.
- Stating objections clearly. Avoiding confrontation if at all possible. Being assertive rather than aggressive. Sticking to the facts and reasserting them if need be.
- All standard procedures should be followed. Supervisors and management should be kept informed at all times.

- Before standard procedures are bypassed, the issue should be presented to the person most concerned with the matter. If it is clear that the evidential material is on record and has been verified and confirmed by independent sources, it may be possible to obtain a positive response. This may involve working through the decision-making process with those concerned.
- Anticipating and documenting any retaliation—the likelihood of some retaliation may be high.

Such a check may reduce the need to report the event beyond the immediate organization concerned, and represents the professional preparations necessary before reporting to an extra-organizational authority. The checklist reinforces the need to avoid conflict throughout the process. If any dispute between the engineer and employing authorities escalates to public disclosure and the involvement of the press, all parties are liable to lose.

Situations may arise where the professional engineer becomes aware of ethical issues only after decisions have been made and implemented. If these involve unsafe or unacceptable practices, then the appropriate public authority should be advised, and the responsibility passed over, going to the highest level of authority if need be. Similarly, if corruption or illegalities have been disclosed, then these also should be reported to the appropriate responsible legal or public sector authority.

It is in the interest of all concerned to have established protocols that enable those involved to address the issues, some of which may start off as expressions of concern, rather than of complaint. Such a protocol requires carefully thought-out complaints and consultation procedures. They would include the following.

- The procedures should stipulate the steps to be taken after the reporter has been unable to take the matter further with his immediate senior manager.
- Recognition that matters are not limited to the individual's own area of responsibility. This provides a reminder that the responsibility of a professional to the safety and well being of society go beyond particular role responsibilities.
- An initial review of the data by competent professionals in the organization. This may be supplemented by the appointment of an independent reviewer, or a panel of reviewers to determine if there is cause for concern and if any more data is required. Responses should be given speedily and communicated to the reporter with the reasons for any decision reached.
- Written records of all transactions should be kept for internal audit, or where a government body might be involved for public inspection, the record should document the concern, the initial response and the assessment of the consequences if this concern is not addressed.

- To assure any originators that the matter is being taken seriously, there must be a mechanisim for a right of appeal to another authority if the finding does not meet the concerns of the reporter. At this point the professional body might be involved, perhaps with a member from a selected panel of senior engineers, who could be given evidence in confidence. The results of this more formal approach would be communicated to the reporter within a defined period.
- There should be the greatest possible transparency at all stages, including prompt feedback to the complainant.
- This entire protocol should be clearly set out in the staff handbook.
- The whole process should be reviewed periodically so that the effects of good practice can be seen and any bad practice modified.

2.7 SUSTAINABILITY

Over recent years, there has been a great increase in the understanding of sustainable development and 'green' issues. Engineering responsibilities for the environment are currently governed by laws controlling environmental matters. Stringent regulations now exist at local, national and international levels. These are designed to ensure that the industry conducts its business in an environmentally friendly fashion. British Standard 7750—*Specification for environmental management,* ISO 14001—*Environmental management systems: specification with guidance for use, and Environmental assessment directive* 85/337/Ec—all provide guidance and control to ensure that projects receive an appropriate level of environmental assessment and analysis. More importantly, these regulations have begun to form a culture in the industry where environmental awareness is at the heart of the project, rather than a late 'add-on'.

Engineers find themselves attempting to rationalize/comply with many conflicting needs and requirements when attempting to realize business projects. Clients may have many outlooks with regard to the environment. For instance:

- They may be part of an organization which intends to 'pay the fine' rather than attempt to use resources on environmental protection considerations.
- It may alternatively be part of an organization that adopts governmental restrictions as a cost of doing business but complies without enthusiasm or commitment.
- They may be part of an enlightened and responsible organization with a wish to incorporate the best environmental considerations.

The actions of the engineer on matters of sustainability and environmental impact are summarized as follows:

1. Engineers must assume a responsibility for the effects of their work and endeavour to make a substantial contribution to the protection of the environment.
2. They must not participate in projects that are unnecessarily destructive to the environment even if these projects do not endanger physical life or health.
3. Engineers should express their professional opinions on environmental matters based on sound knowledge and analysis. They must see to it that personal protests do not overtly conflict with their clients' wishes since this would invite public disrespect and mistrust for the profession.
4. Where no national guidelines exist, the engineer has the responsibility to set appropriate standards to communicate these to others and to work in accordance with these self-generated regulations.
5. Should the engineer consider that the project is unnecessarily harmful to the environment, then he should attempt to explain the situation to his clients. In the event of his opinion being disregarded, the engineer has the right to withdraw from the project, with the right to make his concerns known to the relevant authorities.

2.8 KOHLBERG'S STAGES OF MORAL DEVELOPMENT

Kohlberg felt that people progressed in their moral reasoning through a series of stages. He believed that there were six identifiable stages which could be more generally classified into three levels. Kohlberg's classification can be outlined as in Table 2.1.

Table 2.1 Kohlberg's Six Stages of Moral Development

Level	Stage	Social orientation
Pre-conventional	1	Obedience and punishment
	2	Individualism, instrumentalism, and exchange
Conventional	3	"Good boy/good girl"
	4	Law and order
Post-conventional	5	Social contract
	6	Principled conscience

The first level of moral thinking is that generally found at the elementary school level. In the first stage of this level, people behave according to socially acceptable norms because they are told to do so by some authority figure (e.g., parent or teacher). This obedience is compelled by the threat or application of punishment. The second stage of this level is characterized by a view that right behaviour means acting in one's own best interests. The second level of moral thinking is that generally found in society; hence the name "conventional." The first stage of this level (stage 3) is characterized by an attitude that seeks to do those things that gain the approval of others. The second stage is one oriented to abiding by the law and responding to the obligations of duty. The third level of moral thinking is one that Kohlberg felt is not reached by the majority of adults. Its first stage (stage 5) is an understanding of social mutuality and a genuine interest in the welfare of others. The last stage (stage 6) is based on respect for universal principle and the demands of individual conscience. While Kohlberg always believed in the existence of stage 6 and had some nominees for it, he could never get enough subjects to define it, much less observe their longitudinal movement to it.

Kohlberg believed that individuals could only progress through these stages, one stage at a time. That is, they could not 'jump' stages. They could not, for example, move from an orientation of selfishness to the law and order stage without passing through the good boy and good girl stage. They could only come to a comprehension of a moral rationale, one stage above their own. Thus, according to Kohlberg, it was important to present them with moral dilemmas for discussion approach. He saw this as one of the ways in which moral development can be promoted through formal education. Note that Kohlberg believed that most moral development occurs through social interaction. The discussion approach is based on the insight that individuals develop as a result of cognitive conflicts at their current stage.

First stage. *Personal Survival*—"Me against the world"—No altruism at all. You don't expect anyone to help you. You act upon survival instincts. These people just take what they need without consideration of the impact on others.

Second stage. "You scratch my back, I'll scratch yours". You recognize that others can help you and that you must return the favour!. Still no altruism.

Third stage. *Good or bad behaviour* is dictated by whether it is seen as good or as bad, depending upon whether it conforms or goes against some learned doctrine of acceptable behaviour (peer pressure). Any altruism is only seeking the approval of others.

Fourth stage. *Law and order.* Recognition that behaviour needs to conform to written laws. The law is the final arbiter and is seen as something that should be obeyed without question. Any altruism is seen as a responsibility. Kolberg calls the next two stages "Post Conventional", these stages go beyond the social programming requiring individuals to discover for themselves the "higher morality".

Fifth stage. *The social contract.* Recognition that laws exist for the common good but that these laws must not be viewed as applying in every case. There is a genuine interest in the welfare of others and the concept of justice. *Altruistic*. This stage is typical of those who protest against the inequities of the system, go to jail on social principles, etc.

Sixth stage. *Recognition of universal principles.* The individual fully realizes that there is a "higher law" to which we are all subject. The individual's highly evolved conscience is the sole basis for behaviour. Most behaviours are for the benefit of others. These people are willing to risk their lives for others.

According to Kohlberg, children usually develop through stages 1 and 2 and settle into 3 and 4. A minority of adults pass into the higher stages 5 and 6. Once you understand this theory, it explains a great deal about the varying morality that exists in any society. It also shows the way to elevate others.

2.8.1 Piaget's Theory

Piaget's central claim was that increases in reasoning skill over time were punctuated by shifts in perspective that could only be called qualitative change from one stage (or "type," if you will) of thinking to another. This is a thoroughly cognitive theory).

Ages 7 to 11	Concrete operations	Children can decentre; they acquire the concept of conversion, but they cannot reason abstractly or test hypotheses systematically.
Starts at age 11 or 12	Formal operations	Children begin to reason abstractly.

For Piaget, children start out as concrete and egocentric thinkers (even infants have such thoughts). As they gain more cognitive ability with age, they begin to be able to "decentre" and see things from another perspective. But they are still concrete in their approach to things. More experience and (here is a key) some cognitive reorganization eventually allow most people to become abstract thinkers.

2.9 CAROL GILLIGAN THEORY

Gilligan's work is a complaint against the male centred personality psychology of Freud and Erickson, and the male centred developmental psychology of Kohlberg. Her complaint is not that it is unjust to leave women out of psychology. It is not good psychology if it leaves out half of the human race. Gilligan proposes a stage theory of moral development for women. Much of the research suggests that the stage theories are too simplistic in their picture of changes in skills, attributes, and competencies over time.

Kohlberg applied Piaget's theory to the development of moral thinking. Borrowing from Piaget's "preoperational/concrete/formal" distinctions, Kohlberg came up with the stage theory given in Table 2.2.

Table 2.2 Moral Development—Kohlberg's Stage Theory

Approximate age range	Stage	Substages
Birth to 9	Pre-conventional	• Avoid punishment • Gain reward
Ages 9 to 20	Conventional	• Gain approval and avoid disapproval • Duty and guilt
Age 20+ maybe never	Post-conventional	• Agreed upon rights • Personal moral stands

The pre-conventional moral stage is based on the cognitive abilities of a person in Piaget's concrete operational stage. Moral decisions are egocentric and concrete. So you can see how reward and punishment are the typical bases of reasoning at this stage. The conventional stage is based on the children's ability to "decentre" their moral universe and take the moral perspective of their parents and other important members of society into account. The decision making base on standards are thought to be universalizable and not dependent on culture. Kohlberg's system was based on extensive research he and his students did with interviews in which they asked children and adults to give the reasons they had for moral decisions. So his stages and ages do not correspond exactly from Piaget but a similarity can be seen.

As a student of Kohlberg, Gilligan was taken by the stage theory approach (see Table 2.3) in understanding moral reasoning. But she disagreed with her mentor's assessment of the content of the moral system within which people developed. From her careful interviews with women making momentous decisions in their lives, Gilligan concluded that these women were thinking more about the caring things to do rather than the thing the rules allowed.

Table 2.3 Gilligan's Stages of Cognitive Development

Approximate age range	Stage	Goal
Not listed	Pre-conventional	Goal is individual survival
Transition is from selfishness to responsibility to others		
Not listed	Conventional	Self-sacrifice is goodness
Transition is from goodness to truth that she is a person too		
May be never	Post-conventional	Principle of nonviolence—do not hurt others or self

Thus Gilligan produces her own stage theory of moral development for women. Like Kohlberg's, it has three major divisions: Pre-conventional, conventional, and post-conventional. For Gilligan, the transitions between the stages are fuelled by changes in the sense of self rather than in changes in cognitive capability. Kohlberg's approach is based on Piaget's cognitive developmental model while Gilligan's is based on a modified version of Freud's approach to ego development. Kohlberg built his theory based on interviews with males only. Gilligan has certainly shown the inadequacy of that. In addition, she has demolished the idea that there is only one dimension of moral reasoning. Finally, she has connected back with moral decision making concerns about both the self and the social environment in which the self lives. Her basic claim is that women have no place in these earlier theories and that is why women's development has been considered an aberration from the normal. Women are different, but they are not inferior. Men and women view relationships differently. Current research agrees with Gilligan.

2.10 MORAL DILEMMAS

Moral dilemmas, at the very least, involve conflicts between moral requirements. Consider the following examples.

2.10.1 Examples

In Book I of Plato's *Republic*, Cephalous defines *justice* as speaking the truth and paying one's debts. Socrates quickly refutes this account by suggesting that it would be wrong to repay certain debts—for example, to return a borrowed weapon to a friend who is not in his right mind. Socrates' point is not that repaying debts is without moral import; rather, he wants to show that it is not always right to repay one's debts, at least not exactly when the one to whom the debt is owed demands repayment. What we have here is a conflict between two moral norms: repaying one's debts and protecting others from harm. And in this case, Socrates maintains that protecting others from harm is the norm that takes priority.

Nearly twenty-four centuries later, Jean-Paul Sartre described a moral conflict, the resolution of which was, to many, less obvious than the resolution to the Platonic conflict. Sartre (1957) tells of a student whose brother had been killed in the German offensive of 1940. The student wanted to avenge his brother and to fight forces that he regarded as evil. But the student's mother was living with him, and he was her one consolation in life. The student believed that he had conflicting obligations. Sartre describes him as being torn between two kinds of morality: one of limited scope but certain efficacy, personal devotion to his mother; the other of much wider scope but uncertain efficacy, attempting to contribute to the defeat of an unjust aggressor.

2.10.2 Concept of Moral Dilemma

What is common to the two well-known cases is conflict. In each case, an agent regards herself as having moral reasons to do each of two actions, but doing both actions is not possible. Ethicists have called situations like these *moral dilemmas*. The crucial features of a moral dilemma are these: the agent is required to do each of two (or more) actions; the agent can do each of the actions; but the agent cannot do both (or all) of the actions. The agent thus seems condemned to moral failure; no matter what she does, she will do something wrong (or fail to do something that she ought to do).

The Platonic case strikes many as too easy to be characterized as a genuine moral dilemma. For the agent's solution in that case is clear; it is more important to protect people from harm than to return a borrowed weapon. And in any case, the borrowed item can be returned later, when the owner no longer poses a threat to others. Thus, in this case we can say that the requirement to protect others from serious harm *overrides* the requirement to repay one's debts by returning a borrowed item when its owner so demands. When one of the conflicting requirements overrides the other, we do not have a genuine moral dilemma. So, in addition to the features mentioned above, in order to have a *genuine* moral dilemma it must also be true that neither of the conflicting requirements be overridden.

2.10.3 Problems

It is less obvious in Sartre's case that one of the requirements overrides the other. Why this is so, however, may not be so obvious. Some will say that our uncertainty about what to do in this case is simply the result of uncertainty about the consequences. If we were certain that the student could make a difference in defeating the Germans, the obligation to join the military would prevail. But if the student made little difference whatsoever in that cause, then his obligation to tend to his mother's needs would take precedence since there he is virtually certain to be helpful. Others, though, will say that these obligations are equally weighty, and that uncertainty about the consequences is not at issue here.

Ethicists as diverse as Kant, Mill, and Ross have assumed that an adequate moral theory should not allow for the possibility of genuine moral dilemmas. Only recently—in the last 40 years or so—have philosophers begun to challenge that assumption. And the challenge can take at least two different forms. Some will argue that it is *not possible* to preclude genuine moral dilemmas. Others will argue that even if it were possible, it is *not desirable* to do so.

The conflicts in Plato's case and Sartre's case arose because there is more than one moral precept (using 'precept' to designate rules and principles). More than one precept sometimes applies to the same situation, and in some of these cases the precepts demand conflicting actions. One obvious solution here would be to arrange the precepts, however many there might be, hierarchically. By this scheme, the highest ordered precept always prevails, the second prevails unless it conflicts with the first, and so on.

However, there are at least two ticklish problems with this obvious solution. *First*, it just does not seem credible to hold that moral rules and principles should be hierarchically ordered. While the requirements to keep one's promises and to prevent harm to others can clearly conflict with each other, it is far from clear that one of these requirements should *always* prevail over the other. In the Platonic case, the obligation to prevent harm is clearly stronger.

But there can easily be cases where the harm that can be prevented is relatively mild and the promise that is to be kept is very important. And most other pairs of precepts are like this.

The *second problem* with this easy solution is deeper. Even if it were plausible to arrange moral precepts hierarchically, situations can arise in which the same precept gives rise to conflicting obligations. Perhaps the most widely discussed case of this sort is taken from William Styron's *Sophie's Choice* (1980). Sophie and her two children are at a Nazi concentration camp. A guard confronts Sophie and tells her that one of her children will be allowed to live and one will be killed. But it is Sophie who must decide which child will be killed. Sophie can prevent the death of either of her children, but only by condemning the other to be killed. The guard makes the situation even more excruciating by informing Sophie that if she chooses neither, then both will be killed. With this added factor, Sophie has a morally compelling reason to choose one of her children. But for each child, Sophie has an apparently equally strong reason to save him or her. Thus the same moral precept gives rise to conflicting obligations. Some have called such cases *symmetrical.*

2.10.4 Dilemmas and Consistency

What is troubling is that theories that allow for dilemmas fail to be *uniquely action-guiding*. A theory can fail to be uniquely action-guiding in either of two ways: by not recommending any action in a situation that is moral or by recommending incompatible actions. Theories that generate genuine moral dilemmas fail to be uniquely action-guiding in the latter way. Since at least one of the main points of moral theories is to provide agents with guidance, it is desirable for theories to eliminate dilemmas, at least if doing so is possible.

2.10.5 Moral Residue

Let us return to the case of Sartre's student. Suppose he joins the Free French forces. It is likely that he will experience remorse or guilt for having abandoned his mother. And not only will he experience these emotions, this moral residue, but it is appropriate that he does. Yet, had he stayed with his mother and not joined the Free French forces, he also would have appropriately experienced remorse or guilt. But remorse or guilt is appropriate only if the agent properly believes that he has done something wrong (or failed to do something that he was all-things-considered required to do). Since no matter what the agent does, he will appropriately experience remorse or guilt, then no matter what he does, he will have done something wrong. Thus, the agent faces a genuine moral dilemma.

Many cases of moral conflict are similar to this example. Certainly the case from *Sophie's Choice* fits here. No matter which of her children Sophie saves, she will experience enormous guilt for the consequences of that choice. Indeed, if Sophie did not experience such guilt, we would think that there was something morally wrong with her. In these cases, proponents of the argument (for dilemmas) from moral residue must claim that four things are true: (1) when the agents acts, she experiences remorse or guilt; (2) that she experiences these emotions is appropriate and called for; (3) had the agent acted on the other of the conflicting requirements, she would also have experienced remorse or guilt; and (4) in the latter case, these emotions would have been equally appropriate and called for. In these situations, then, remorse or guilt will be appropriate no matter what the agent does, and these emotions are appropriate only when the agent has done something wrong. Therefore, these situations are genuinely dilemmatic.

All of this suggests that there are situations in which an agent's remorse or guilt is not inappropriate even though the agent has done nothing wrong. Because of this and because in any given situation the appropriate response may be regret and not remorse, opponents of dilemmas have a way to respond to the argument that appeals to the appropriateness of remorse.

2.11 TYPES OF MORAL DILEMMAS

One distinction is between *epistemic* conflicts and *ontological* conflicts. The former involve conflicts between two (or more) moral requirements and the agent does not know which of the conflicting requirements takes precedence in her situation. Everyone concedes that there can be situations where one requirement does take priority over the other with which it conflicts, though at the time action is called for, it is difficult for the agent to tell which requirement prevails. The latter are conflicts between two (or more) moral requirements, and neither is overridden. This is not simply because the agent does not *know* which requirement is stronger—neither is. Genuine moral dilemmas, if there are any, are ontological. Both opponents and supporters of dilemmas acknowledge that there are epistemic conflicts.

Another distinction is between *self-imposed* moral dilemmas and dilemmas imposed on an agent *by the world*, as it were. Former type of conflicts arise because of the agent's own wrongdoing. If an agent made two promises that he knew were in conflict, then, through his own actions he created a situation in which it is not possible for him to discharge both of his requirements. Dilemmas imposed on the agent by the world, by contrast, do not arise because of the agent's wrongdoing. The case of Sartre's student is an example, as is the case from *Sophie's Choice*. For supporters of dilemmas, this distinction is not all that important. But among opponents of dilemmas, there is a disagreement about whether the distinction is important. Some of these opponents hold that self-imposed dilemmas are possible, but that their existence does not point to any deep flaws in moral theory. Moral theory tells agents how they ought to behave; but if agents violate moral norms, things can go askew.

Other opponents deny that even self-imposed dilemmas are possible. They argue that an adequate moral theory should tell agents what they ought to do in their current circumstances regardless of how those circumstances arose. And given the prevalence of wrongdoing, if a moral theory did not issue uniquely action-guiding "contrary-to-duty imperatives", it would be severely lacking.

Yet another distinction is between *obligation dilemmas* and *prohibition dilemmas*. The former are situations in which more than one feasible action is obligatory. The latter involve cases in which all feasible actions are forbidden; argue that plausible principles of deontic logic may well render obligation dilemmas impossible; but they do not preclude the possibility of prohibition dilemmas. The case of Sartre's student, if genuinely dilemmatic, is an obligation dilemma; Sophie's case is a prohibition dilemma.

There is another reason that friends of dilemmas emphasize this distinction. Some think that the "disjunctive solution" used by opponents of dilemmas — when equally strong precepts conflict, the agent is required to act on one or the other—is much more plausible when applied to obligation dilemmas than when applied to prohibition dilemmas.

2.12 MORAL AUTONOMY

Autonomy literally means, "self-determining" or "independent". But not just any kind of independent reflection about ethics amounts to moral autonomy. Moral autonomy can be viewed as the skill and habit of thinking rationally about ethical issues on the basis of moral concern. This foundation of moral concern, or general responsiveness to moral values, derives primarily from the training we receive as children in being sensitive to the needs and rights of others (as well as of ourselves). Where such training is absent, as it often is with abused or neglected children, the tragic result can be an adult sociopath capable of murdering without compunction. Sociopaths, who, by definition lack a sense of moral concern and guilt, are never morally autonomous—no matter how independent their intellectual reasoning about ethics maybe.

Moral autonomy can be accomplished by improving various practical skills that will help produce effective independent thought about moral issues. As related to engineering ethics these skills include the following:

1. Proficiency in recognizing moral problems and issues in engineering. This involves being able to distinguish them from, as well as relate them to, problems in law, economics, religious doctrine, or the descriptions of physical systems.
2. Skill in comprehending, clarifying and critically assessing arguments on opposing side of moral issues.
3. The ability to form consistent and comprehensive viewpoints based upon consideration of relevant facts.

4. Imaginative awareness of alternative responses to the issues and creative solutions for practical difficulties.
5. Sensitivity to genuine difficulties and subtleties. This includes a willingness to undergo and tolerate some uncertainty in making troublesome moral judgements or decisions.
6. Enhanced precision in the use of a common ethical language which is necessary to be able to express and defend one's moral views adequately to others.
7. Better appreciation of both the possibilities of using rational dialogue in resolving moral conflicts and of the need for tolerance of difference in perspective among morally reasonable people.
8 Awakened sense of the importance of integrating one's professional life and personal convictions, that is, the importance of maintaining one's moral integrity.

Viewing engineering as social experimentation can help restore a sense of autonomous participation in one's work. As an experimenter, an engineer is exercising the sophisticated training that forms the core of his identity as a professional. Moreover, viewing an engineering project as an experiment that can result in unknown consequences should help inspire a critical and questioning attitude about the adequacy of current economic and safety standards. This can also lead to a greater sense of personal involvement with one's work.

The attitude of management plays a decisive role in how much moral autonomy engineers feel they have. It would be in the long term interest of a high technology firm to grant its engineers a great deal of latitude in exercising their professional judgement on moral issues relevant to their jobs. But the yardsticks by which a manager's performance is judged on a quarterly or yearly basis often discourage this. This is particularly true in our age of conglomerates, when annual profitability is more important than consistent quality and long-term retention of satisfied customers. Accordingly, engineers are compelled to look on their professional societies and other outside organizations for moral support. Yet it is no exaggeration to claim that the blue-collar worker with union backing has greater leverage at present in exercising moral autonomy than do many employed professionals. A steel plant worker, for instance, who refused to dump oil into a river in an unauthorized manner was threatened with dismissal, but his union saw to it that the threat was never carried out. Or take the case of the automobile plant inspector who repeatedly warned his supervisors about poorly welded panels that allowed carbon monoxide from the exhaust to leak into the cab. Receiving no satisfactory response from the company, he blew the whistle. The company wanted to fire him, but pressure from the union allowed him to keep his job.

Professional societies, originally organized as learned societies dedicated to the exchange of technical information, lack comparable power to protect their members, although most engineers have no other group to rely on for such protection. Only now is the need for moral and legal support of members in the exercise of their professional obligations being recognized by those societies.

2.13 MORAL DISAGREEMENT

Abortion, surrogacy, euthanasia, the death penalty, racism, sexism, homosexuality, world hunger, animal rights, and environmental issues are all areas characterized by fundamental disagreements—often intense, sometimes bitter and acrimonious. This situation is made even more perplexing by the fact that in all these debates, each side has good arguments in support of its position. Ultimately, these are disagreements among intelligent people of good will. And it is precisely this fact that makes them so disturbing. Certainly, part of moral disagreement can be attributed to ignorance or ill will, but the troubling part is the moral disagreement among informed and benevolent people.

2.14 MORAL ABSOLUTISM

Moral absolutists are not confined to a single position. Some absolutists believe in communism, others believe just as absolutely in free market economics. Some moral philosophers are absolutists, believing that their moral viewpoint is the only legitimate one. But what characterized all absolutists is the conviction that their truth is the truth. The first, and perhaps the most common response to such disagreements, is to claim that there is a single, ultimate answer to the questions being posed. This is the answer of the absolutists, those who believe there is a single Truth with a capital "T." Usually, absolutists claim to know what that truth is and it usually corresponds, not surprisingly, to their own position.

Moral absolutists are not confined to a single position. Indeed, absolutism is best understood as much as a way of *holding* certain beliefs as it is an item of such belief. Religious fundamentalists—whether Christian, Muslim, Hindu or any other—are usually absolutists. Some moral philosophers are absolutists, believing that their moral viewpoint is the only legitimate one. But what characterized all absolutists is the conviction that their truth is *the* truth.

Moral absolutist may be right, but there are good reasons to be skeptical about their claims. If they are right, how do they explain the persistence of moral disagreement? Certainly, there are disagreements and disputes in other areas (including the natural sciences), but in ethics there seems to be persistence to these disputes that we usually do not find in other areas. It is hard to explain this from an absolutist standpoint without saying such disagreement is due to ignorance or ill will. Absolutists are unable to make sense out of the fact that sometimes we have genuine moral disagreements among well-informed and good-intentioned people who are honestly and openly seeking the truth.

2.15 MORAL RELATIVISM

Moral relativists maintain that moral disagreements stem from the fact that what is right for one is not necessarily right for another. Morality, they claim, is purely relative, just as beauty lies in the eyes of the beholder and is relative. There is no ultimate standard in terms of which perspectives can be judged. No one is wrong, everyone is right within his or her own sphere. Just to admit that moral disagreement exists is called descriptive relativism, and this is a comparatively uncontroversial claim. There is plenty of disagreement in the moral realm, just as there is in most other areas of life. However, normative relativists go further. They not only maintain that such disagreement exists, they also say that each is right relative to his or her own culture. Incidentally, it is also worth noting that relativists disagree about precisely what morality is relative to. At the one end of the spectrum are those (cultural moral relativists) who say that morality is relative to culture, and at the other end of the spectrum are those (moral subjectivists) who argue that morality is relative to each individual.

2.16 MORAL PLURALISM

Absolutism fails to offer a convincing account of how opposing people could be both well informed and good intentioned. Relativism fails to offer a convincing account of how people can agree. It says no one is wrong, that each culture (or individual) is right unto itself. However, it offers no help about how to resolve these moral disputes. Moral pluralists maintain that there are moral truths, but they do not form a body of coherent and consistent truths in the way that one finds in science or mathematics. Moral truths are real, but partial. Moreover, they are inescapably plural. There are many more truths, not just one and they may conflict with one another. Moral absolutists are analogous to old-fashioned monarchists; there is one leader, and he or she has the absolute truth. Moral relativists are closer to anarchists: each person or group has its own truth.

2.17 MORALITY AS CONSEQUENCE

What makes an action morally good? For many of us, what counts are *consequences*. The right action is the one that produces good consequences. If I give money to Oxfam to help starving people, and if Oxfam saves the lives of starving people and helps them develop a self-sustaining economy, then I have done something good. It is good because it produces good consequences. For this reason, it is the right thing to do. Those who subscribe to this position are called *consequentialists*. All consequentialists share a common belief that it is consequences that make an action good, but they differ among themselves about precisely which consequences.

2.18 ETHICAL EGOISM

Some consequentialists, called ethical egoists, maintain that each of us should look only at the consequences that affect us. In their eyes, each person ought to perform those actions that contribute most to their own self-interest. Each person is the best judge of their own self-interest, and each person is responsible for maximizing their own self-interest.

Ethical egoism has been criticised on a number of counts, most notably, that it simply draws the circle of morality much too closely around the isolated individual. Critics maintain that self-interest is precisely what morality has to overcome, not what it should espouse. Egoism preaches selfishness, but morality should encourage altruism, compassion, love, and a sense of community—all, beyond the reach of the egoist.

2.19 FEMINIST CONSEQUENTIALISM

During the last twenty years, much interesting and valuable work has been done in the area of feminist ethics. It would be misleading to think of feminist approaches to ethics as falling into a single camp, but certainly some feminist moral philosophers have sketched out consequentialist accounts of the moral life in at least two different ways. *First*, some feminists have argued that morality is a matter of consequences, but the consequences are not best understood or evaluated in the traditional computational model offered by utilitarianism. Instead, they focus primarily on the ways in which particular actions have consequences for relationships and feelings. Negative consequences are those that destroy relationships and hurt others, especially those that hurt others emotionally. Within this tradition, the morally good course of action is the one that preserves the greatest degree of connectedness among all those affected by it. *Second*, other feminists have accepted a roughly utilitarian account of consequences, but have paid particular attention to the consequences that affect women. Such consequences, they argue, have often been overlooked by traditional utilitarian calculators, supposedly impartial but often insensitive to the harm done to women.

2.20 CONFORMITY TO GOD'S COMMANDS

There are two principal difficulties with this approach: one external, and the other internal. The external problem is that, while this may provide a good reason for believers to act in particular ways, it hardly gives a persuasive case to non-believers. The internal difficulty is that it is often difficult, even with the best of intentions, to discern what God's commands actually are. Sacred texts, for example, contain numerous injunctions, but it is rare that any religious tradition takes *all* of them seriously. How do we decide which injunctions to take seriously and which to ignore or interpret metaphorically?

2.21 PROPER INTENTION

Intentions are often built into our vocabulary for describing actions. The difference between stabbing a person and performing surgery on that person may well reside primarily in the intention of the agent. A sense of duty, universalizability, a respect for other persons, sincerity or authenticity, care and compassion—these are but a few of the acceptable moral motivations. Consider, first of all, the motive of duty. Immanuel Kant argued that what gives an action moral worth is that it is done for the sake of duty. In his eyes, the morally admirable person is the one who, despite inclinations to the contrary, does the right thing solely because it is *the right thing* to do. The person who contributes to charities out of a sense of duty is morally far superior to the person who does the same thing in order to look good in the eyes of others, despite the fact that the consequences may be the same in both cases.

2.22 UNIVERSALIZABILITY

Kant suggested an important test whether our understanding of duty was rational in any particular instance. We always act with a subjective rule or maxim that guides our decision. Is this maxim that everyone accepts, or is it one that fails this test of universalizability? If you cheat in an exam, it's like lying: you are saying something is your work when it is not. Imagine you cheat in all the exams in a course and finish with an average of 98%. The professor then gives you a grade of "D." You storm into the professor's office, demanding an explanation. The professor calmly says, "Oh, I lied in the grade sheet." Your natural reply would be: "But you can't lie about my grade!" Kant's point is that, by cheating, you've denied the validity of your own claim. You've implicitly said that it is morally all right for people to lie. But of course you don't believe it's permissible for your professor to lie—only for you yourself to do so. This, Kant says, fails the test of universalizability. You cannot approve of your own lying without approving of everyone else's, and yet the advantage you get depends precisely on other people's honesty. It is the irrationality of making an exception of my own lying in this way that Kant feels violates the moral law.

2.23 RESPECT FOR OTHER PERSONS

We should never treat people merely as things, Kant argued. Rather, we should always respect them as autonomous (self-directing) moral agents. Both capitalism and technology pressure us to treat people merely as things, and many have found Kant's refusal to do this to be of crucial moral importance. We use people merely as things when we do not let them make their own decisions and when we harm them for our own benefit without respect for their rights. Consider the now infamous Tuskegee experiment, in which medical researchers tracked the development of syphilis in a group of African-American men for over 30 years, never telling them the precise nature of their disease and never treating them—something which would have been both expensive and effective. Instead, the researchers let the disease proceed through its ultimate fatal course in order to observe more closely the details of its progress. These men were used merely as means to the researchers' ends.

2.24 CARING

Many philosophers have argued that caring about other persons is the heart of the moral life, and that a morality of care leads to a refreshingly new picture of morality as centring on relationships, feelings, and connectedness rather than impartiality, justice, and fairness. The justice-oriented person in a moral dispute will ask what the fair thing to do is, and then proceed to follow that course of action, no matter what effect that has on others. The care-oriented individual, on the other hand, will try to find the course of action which best preserves the interests of all involved and which does the least amount of damage to the relationships involved.

2.25 RESPECT FOR RIGHTS

What specific aspects of other persons ought we to respect? The Bill of Rights was the first set of amendments to the United States Constitution. At approximately the same time, the French were drafting the Declaration of the Rights of Man and Citizen. Concern for human rights has continued well into the twentieth century, and the last 40 years in the United States have been marked by an intense concern with rights—the civil rights movement for racial equality, the equal rights movement for women, the animal rights movement, the gay rights movement, and equal rights for Americans with disabilities. Rights provide the final criterion to be considered here for evaluating acts. Those acts which violate basic human rights are morally wrong, this tradition suggests. Torture, imprisonment and executing the innocent, denial of the right to vote, denial of due process—these are all instances of actions that violate human rights. (The fact that an act does not violate basic human rights does not mean that it is morally unobjectionable; there may be other criteria for evaluating it as well as rights.) Human rights, defenders of this tradition maintain, are not subject to nationality, race, religion, class, or any other such limitation. They cannot be set aside for reasons of utility, convenience, or political or financial gain. We possess them simply by virtue of being human beings, and they thus exhibit a universality that provides the foundation for a global human community.

Criticisms of the rights tradition abound. First, how do we determine *which* rights we have? Rights theorists often respond that we have a right to those things—such as life, freedom, and property—which are necessary to human existence itself. Yet many claim that such necessities are contextual, not universal, and there is something logically fallacious about proceeding from the claim that I need something to the claim that I have a right to it. Needs, these critics argue, do not entail rights. Second, critics have asked whether these rights are negative rights (i.e., freedom from certain kinds of interference) or positive rights (i.e., entitlements). Finally, some critics have argued that the current focus on rights has obscured other, morally relevant aspects of our lives. Rights establish a moral minimum for the ways in which we interact with others, especially strangers we do not care about. But when we are dealing with those we know and care about, more may be demanded of us morally than just respecting their rights.

2.26 CONTRAST BETWEEN ACT-ORIENTED AND CHARACTER-ORIENTED ETHICS

This Aristotelian approach to ethic, sometimes called character ethics or virtue ethics, is distinctive. In contrast to the preceding act-oriented approaches, it does not focus on what makes *acts* right or wrong. Rather, it focuses on *people* and their moral character. Instead of asking, "What should I do?" those in this tradition ask, "What kind of person should I strive to be?" This gives a very different focus to the morality.

A similar situation exists in ethics. We need good rules and the preceding sections have described some attempts to articulate those rules. But we also need good people to have the wisdom and good will to interpret and apply those rules. Far from being in conflict with each other, act-oriented and character-oriented approaches to ethics complement one another.

2.27 VIRTUE OF COURAGE

Aristotle analyzes courage primarily in military terms, but we now see that it is a virtue necessary to a wide range of human activities—and those who lack courage will rarely flourish. Courage is the strength of character to face and overcome that which we fear. Fears differ from one person to the other, but we all have them. Some may fear physical danger; some may fear intimacy and the psychological vulnerability that comes with it; some may fear commitment; some may fear taking risks to gain what they desire.

Imagine people who lack the courage to take chances in their careers. They desire a more challenging position, but they are unwilling to give up the old position in order to make the move. Imagine those who fear the vulnerability that comes with genuinely intimate relationships. They long for intimacy, but are unable or unwilling to take the risk necessary to attain it. Those who lack courage will be unable to take the necessary risks, and this is the sense in which cowardice is a vice: it prevents us from flourishing. Virtues are usually a mean between two extremes. One of the extremes here is clear: cowardice. But what would it mean to be very courageous? First, one could be willing to risk too quickly. Rashness is one way of having too much courage. Or one could risk much for too little. To run into a burning building to save a trapped child is courage; to run into the same building to save an old pair of shoes is foolhardy. Foolhardiness is another way of having too much courage.

2.28 COMPASSION

First, let us define compassion and bracket it between its two extremes, the vices that correspond to a deficiency or an excess of compassion. Compassion itself is a feeling for our fellow moral beings (human beings and perhaps animals). It is literally a "feeling with…" an ability to identify with the feelings of another being, especially feelings of suffering. Moreover, it is usually oriented toward action. The compassionate person is moved to help those who are suffering, and we would doubt the genuineness of the compassion if it never led to action. Those with too little compassion are cold hearted, indifferent to the suffering of others. Yet what is "too much" compassion? Presumably, it is being overly concerned with the suffering of others. There are several ways in which this could occur. First, we might be so concerned with the suffering of others that we neglect ourselves and those to whom we have direct duties. Second, we might be so concerned with the suffering of others that we neglect the non-suffering parts of their personality, turning them into pure victims when they are not. Third, we may be rightly concerned with the suffering of others, but we may manifest this in inappropriate ways. If compassion for a child crying in pain during a medical procedure leads us to kidnap the child to save it from suffering, we have expressed our compassion in an inappropriate way.

Compassion has an emotional element to it, but it is not just a blind feeling. Rather, it is also a way of perceiving the world—the world looks different through the eyes of the compassionate person than through the eyes of the sociopath. Moreover, it is also a way of thinking about the world, a way of understanding it. Compassion has to make judgements about the nature and causes of suffering and also about the possible remedies for suffering. Compassion, finally, is also a way of acting, a way of responding to the sufferings of the world. Compassion can be both deeply passionate and smart at the same time. We also have to know how to respond to suffering in effective ways that not only relieve the immediate suffering but also help the sufferers to free themselves from future suffering. Compassion needs to be wise, not just strongly felt.

2.29 VALUE BASED ETHICS

How does a corporation determine ethical standards of behaviour, and then communicate those standards, to hundreds or thousands of employees? Throughout the global marketplace, corporations are looking for effective tools to help managers and employees make decisions that reflect their company's values, ethical standards, and strategic direction. Implementing value-based ethics approaches is a continuous process, requiring ongoing commitment, cumulative messages, and periodic evaluation and redirection. The approach to each initiative involves four key stages: Assessment, Awareness, Integration, and Evaluation.

Assessment. The primary goal of the Assessment stage is to identify the gap between stated corporate values and the way those values are put into practice (or not put into practice) in daily employee behaviours. Some of the areas include:

- Corporate culture
- Factors that positively influence employee behaviour (Values drivers)
- Factors that negatively impact employee behaviour (Organizational barriers)
- Current/Previous corporate training
- Current/Previous ethics/Compliance activities
- Assessment culminates with a statement of short and long-term goals, and a development and implementation plan.

Awareness. Awareness does not mean a one-time event, a poster in the cafeteria or a letter in a paycheck. Awareness of ethics must become a permanent part of a company's culture. High profile, corporate-wide awareness efforts increase the visibility of ethics policies, staff, and resources by combining marketing, learning, and communication strategies in tools and training. Initial awareness elements introduce the concept of values-based ethics and establish employee expectations. In subsequent cycles, awareness elements build on earlier ones, with more sophisticated topics such as decision-making, mishap prevention, and corporate reputation.

Integration. The key to closing the gap between values in a Mission Statement and values in action is to align employee behaviour around common organizational goals. Only by integrating values based approaches into all work processes can an ethics initiative change employee behaviours. The existing management training programmes such as supply chain management, are natural vehicles for values integration, management and leadership training programs on trust building and role modelling can also support value-based ethics by addressing organizational barriers.

Evaluation. Measurement tools that gauge the extent to which objectives have been achieved provide the necessary information to set new goals for the next cycle. Success is defined as narrowing the gap between stated values and employee behaviour. Some of the ways of evaluating the success of an ethics initiative include:

- Employee focus groups during programme development
- Participant evaluation forms
- Bi-annual employee surveys

Chapter 3

Engineering as Social Experimentation

All products of technology present some potential dangers, and thus engineering is an inherently risky activity. In order to underscore this fact and help in exploring its ethical implications, engineering should be viewed as an experimental process. It is not an experiment conducted solely in laboratory controlled conditions. It is an experiment on a social scale involving human subjects. Experimentation is commonly recognized to play an essential role in the design process. Preliminary tests or simulations are conducted from the time it is decided to convert a new engineering concept into its first rough design. Materials and processes are tried out, usually employing formal experimental techniques. Such tests serve as the basis for more detailed designs which, in turn, are tested. At the production stage, further tests are run until a finished product evolves. The normal design process is thus iterative, carried out on trial designs, with modifications being made on the basis of feedback information acquired from tests. Beyond those specific tests and experiments, however, each engineering project, taken as a totality, may itself be viewed as an experiment.

3.1 COMPARISON WITH STANDARD EXPERIMENTS

Similarities. Several features of engineering practice make it appropriate to view engineering projects as experiments.

1. Any project is carried out in partial ignorance. There are uncertainties in the abstract model used for the design calculations. There are uncertainties in the precise characteristics of materials being processed and fabricated. There are uncertainties about the nature of the stresses the finished product will encounter. Engineers do not have the luxury of waiting until all the relevant factors are in before commencing work. At some point, theoretical exploration and laboratory testing must be by-passed for the sake of moving ahead on a project. Indeed,

one talent crucial to an engineer's success lies precisely in the ability to accomplish tasks with only partial knowledge of scientific laws about nature and society.

2. The final outcomes of engineering projects, like those of experiments, are generally uncertain. Often, in engineering, it is not even known what the possible outcomes may be and great risks may attend even seemingly benign projects. A reservoir may do damage to a region's social fabric or to its ecosystem. It may not even serve the intended purpose if the dam leaks or bursts. An aqueduct may bring about a population explosion in a region where it is the only source of water, creating dependency and vulnerability without adequate safeguards. An aircraft may become a status symbol that ultimately bankrupts its owners. A special purpose fingerprint reader may find its main application in the identification and surveillance of dissidents by totalitarian regimes. A nuclear reactor, the scaled-up version of a successful smaller model, may exhibit unexpected problems that endanger the surrounding population, leading to its untimely shutdown at great cost to the owner and the consumers alike. A hair dryer may expose the unknowing or unwary user to lung damage from the asbestos insulation in its barrel.
3. Effective engineering relies upon knowledge gained about products, both before and after they leave the factory. That is, ongoing success in engineering depends upon gaining new knowledge, just like ongoing success in experimentation. Monitoring is thus as essential to engineering as it is to experimentation in general. To monitor is to make periodic observation and tests in order to check for both successful performance and unintended side effects. But since the ultimate test of a product's efficiency, safety, cost-effectiveness, environmental impact, and aesthetic value lies in how well that product functions within the society, monitoring cannot be restricted to the in-house development or testing phases of an engineering venture. It also extends to the stage of client use, as in the case of experimentation where the intermediate and final results of an engineering project deserve analysis if the correct lessons are to be learned from it.

Contrasts. Undoubtedly, engineering differs in some respects from standard experimentation. Some of those very differences help highlight the engineer's special responsibilities. And exploring the differences can also aid our thinking about the moral responsibilities of all those engaged in engineering.

1. There is one great difference in experimental control in a standard experiment. This involves the selection, at random, of members for two different groups. The members of one group receive the special experimental treatment. Members of the other group, called the control group, do not receive that special treatment although they are subjected

to the same environment as the first group in every other respect. In engineering, this is not the usual practice, unless the project is confined to laboratory experimentation because the experimental subjects are human beings, out of the experimenter's control. Indeed, clients and consumers exercise most of the control because it is they who choose the product or item they wish to use. This makes it impossible to obtain a random selection of participants from various groups. Nor can parallel control groups be established based on random sampling. Thus, it is not possible to study the effect of variables on two or more comparison groups, and one must work with the available historical data about the various groups that use the product. There are other fields where it is not uncommon to speak of experiments whose original purpose was not experimental in nature and that involve no control groups.

2. Viewing engineering as an experiment on a social scale, places the focus on the human beings affected by technology and not on inanimate objects. In this respect, engineering closely parallels medical testing of new drugs and techniques on human subjects. Society has recently come to recognize the primacy of the subject's safety and freedom of choice as to whether to participate in medical experiments. Ever since the revelation of prison and concentration camp horrors in the name of medicine, an increasing number of moral and legal safeguards have arisen to ensure that subjects in experiments participate on the basis of informed consent. While the current medical practice increasingly tend to accept as fundamental the subject's moral and legal rights to give informed consent before participating in experiments, contemporary engineering practice is only beginning to recognize those rights. Informed consent is understood as including two main elements: *Knowledge* and *voluntariness*. *First*, subjects should be given not only the information they request but all the information needed to make a reasonable decision. *Second*, subjects must enter into the experiments without being subjected to force, fraud or deception. Respect for the fundamental rights of dissenting minorities and compensation for harmful effects are taken for granted here.
3. The mere purchase of a product does not constitute informed consent. The public and clients must be given information about the practical risks and benefits of the process or product in terms they can understand. Supplying complete information is neither necessary nor in most cases possible. Management is often understandably reluctant to provide more information than current laws require information, fearing disclosure to potential competitors and exposure to potential law suits. Moreover, clients or the public may not be interested in all the relevant information about an engineering project, at least, not until a crisis looms. It is important, nevertheless, that all avenues for disseminating such information be kept open and ready.

3.2 KNOWLEDGE GAINED

Scientific experiments are conducted to gain new knowledge while "engineering projects are experiments that are not necessarily designed to produce very much knowledge". When we carry out an engineering activity as if it were an experiment, we are primarily preparing ourselves for an unexpected outcome. The best outcome is one that tells us nothing new but merely affirms that we are right about something. Unexpected outcome sends us on a search for new knowledge. For the purposes of our model, the distinction is not vital because we are concerned about the manner in which the experiment is conducted, such as the valid consent of human subjects is sought, safety measures are taken, and means exist for terminating the experiment at any time, and providing all participants a safe exit.

3.3 CONSCIENTIOUSNESS

People act responsibly to the extent that they conscientiously commit themselves to live according to moral values. Moral values transcend a consuming preoccupation with a narrowly conceived self-interest. Accordingly, individuals who think solely of their own good to the exclusion of the good of others are not moral agents. By conscientious moral commitment, we mean a sensitivity to the full range of moral values and responsibilities that are relevant to a given situation, and the willingness to develop the skill and expend the effort needed to reach the best balance possible among those considerations. Conscientiousness implies conscientiousness (in the sense of awareness), because intent is not sufficient. Open eyes, open ears, and an open mind are required to recognize a given situation, its implications, and who is involved or affected.

The contemporary working conditions of engineers tend to narrow moral vision solely to the obligations that accompany employee status. As stated earlier, some 90 per cent of engineers are salaried employees, most of whom work within large bureaucracies under great pressure to function smoothly within the organization. There are obvious benefits in terms of prudent self-interest and concern for one's family that make it easy to emphasize as primary the obligations to one's employer. Gradually, the minimal negative duties, such as not falsifying data, not violating patent rights, and not breaching confidentiality, may come to be viewed as the full extent of moral aspiration.

Conceiving engineering as social experimentation restores the vision of engineers as guardians of public interest, whose professional duty it is to guard the welfare and safety of those affected by engineering projects. And this helps ensure that such safety and welfare will not be disregarded in the quest for new knowledge, the rush for profits, a narrow adherence to rules, or a concern over benefits for the many, which ignores harm to the few.

The role of the social guardian should not suggest that engineers force, paternalistically, their own views of the social good upon society. For, as with medical experimentation on humans, the social experimentation involved in engineering should be restricted by the participant's consent—voluntary and informed consent.

3.4 RELEVANT INFORMATION

Conscientiousness is blind without relevant factual information. Hence, showing moral concern involves a commitment to obtain and properly assess all available information pertinent to meeting one's moral obligation. This means, as a first step, fully grasping the context of one's work, which makes it count as an activity having a moral import. Another way of blurring the context of one's work results from the ever increasing specialization and division of labour that makes it easy to think of someone else in the organization as responsible for what otherwise might be a bothersome personal problem. For example, a company may produce items with obsolescence built into them, or items might promote unnecessary energy usage. It is easy to place the burden on the sales department: "Let them inform the customers—if the customers ask". It may be natural thus to rationalize one's neglect of safety or cost considerations; however, it shows no moral concern. While regarding engineering as social experimentation, it also urges the engineer to review his specialized activities in a project as part of a larger whole having a social impact—an impact that may involve a variety of unintended effects. Accordingly, it emphasizes the need for the wide training in disciplines related to engineering and its results as well as the need for a constant effort to imaginatively foresee dangers.

3.5 LEARNING FROM THE PAST

It might be expected that engineers would learn not only from their own earlier designs and operating results but also from those of other engineers. Unfortunately, that is frequently not the case. Lack of established channels of communication, misplaced pride in not asking for information, embarrassment at failure or fear of litigation and plain neglect often impede the flow of such information and lead to many repetitions of past mistakes. Two examples are now given:

1. *The Titanic* lacked a sufficient number of lifeboats: decades later, most of the passengers and crew on the steamship *Arctic* had perished because of the same problem.
2. Valves are notorious for being among the least reliable components of hydraulic systems. It was a pressure relief valve, and lack of definitive information regarding its open or shut state, which contributed to the nuclear reactor accident at Three Mile Island in March 28, 1979. Similar malfunctions had occurred with identical valves on

> nuclear reactors at other locations. The required reports had been filed with Babcock and Wilcox, the reactor's manufacturer, but no attention was given to the problem.

These examples illustrate why it is not sufficient for engineers to rely on hand books alone. Engineering, just like experimentation, demands practitioners to remain alert and well informed at every stage of the project's history.

3.6 ENGINEERS AS MANAGERS, CONSULTANTS, AND LEADERS

Many engineers move into management, often after only a few years in their career. As managers, they are responsible for establishing and maintaining a moral climate conducive to professional responsibility, and also a climate for dealing constructively with conflicts. For profit corporations must seek to make a reasonable profit for stockholders, but they also have responsibilities to employees, customers, clients, and the general public—all of whom are stakeholders in corporations.

Consulting engineers have greater freedom than most salaried engineers. They also must deal with a wider variety of moral concerns since they are responsible for their own business decisions. Honesty in advertising may be difficult to maintain in the face of pressures to promote their business. Controversy still surrounds the legitimacy of competitive bidding and accepting contingency fees. And special problems arise in determining the extent of responsibility in such areas as making safety inspections and arriving at ways to settle disputes.

The important task of consulting within adversarial contests raises special ethical concerns. Engineers serving as expert witnesses in the judicial system are regarded by the courts as responsible for being impartial, in honestly setting forth their professional judgements. Yet being paid by the attorney for one side of the dispute, combined with the desire for additional consulting in the future can create biases and conflicts of interest that may be difficult to deal with honestly. Engineers who are hired as advisors in public planning and policy-making must take special pains to avoid similar biases.

There is an ongoing need for moral leadership in engineering, as in other professions. A primary forum for that leadership is substantial involvement in professional societies which, in addition to furthering technical knowledge and representing engineers collectively, help establish high standards of moral integrity within the profession. Another forum for moral leadership is in community service. Moral leadership does not consist of moral elitism and dominance but, instead, moral creativity in helping to guide, organize, and stimulate groups toward morally desirable goals.

3.7 ACCOUNTABILITY

Too often the term 'accountable' is understood in the narrow sense of being culpable and blameworthy for misdeeds. But more properly it refers to the general disposition of being willing to submit one's actions to moral scrutiny and be open and responsive to the assessments of others. It involves a willingness to present morally cogent reasons for one's conduct when called upon to do so in appropriate circumstances. Submission to an employer's authority, or any authority for that matter, creates in many people a narrow sense of accountability for the consequences of their actions. This was documented by some famous experiments conducted by Stanley Milgram during the 1960s. Subjects would come to a laboratory believing they were to participate in a memory and learning test. In one variation two other people were involved, the "experimenter" and the "learner". The experimenter was regarded by the subject as an authority figure, representing the scientific community. He would give the subject orders to administer electric shocks were to be increased in magnitude with each memory failure. All this, however, was a deception, a "setup". There were no real shocks, and the apparent "learner" and the experimenter" were merely acting parts in a ruse designed to see how far the unknowing experimental subject was willing to go in following orders from an authority figure. The results were astounding. When the subjects were placed in an adjoining room separated from the "learner" by a shaded glass window, more than half were willing to follow orders to the full extent giving the maximum electric jolt of 450 volts. This was in spite of seeing the "learner" who was strapped on to a chair, writhing in apparent agony. The same results occurred when the subjects were allowed to hear the (apparently) pained screams and protests of the "learner", screams and protests that became intense from 130 volts on. There was a striking difference, however, when subjects were placed in the same room within touching distance of the "learner". Then the number of subjects willing to continue to the maximum shock dropped by one-half.

Milgram explained these results by citing a strong psychological tendency in people to be willing to abandon personal accountability when placed under authority. He saw his subjects ascribing all initiative, and thereby all accountability, to what they viewed as legitimate authority. And he noted that the closer the physical proximity, the more difficult it becomes to divest oneself of personal accountability. The divorce between causal influence and moral accountability is common in business and the professions, and engineering is no exception. Such a psychological schism is encouraged by several prominent features of contemporary engineering practice.

1. Large-scale engineering projects involve fragmentation of work. Each person makes only a small contribution to something much larger. Moreover, the final product is often physically removed from one's immediate workplace, creating the kind of "distancing" that Milgram identified as encouraging a lessened sense of personal accountability.

2. Corresponding to the fragmentation of work is a vast diffusion of accountability within large institutions. The often massive bureaucracies within which most engineers work are designed to diffuse and delimit areas of personal accountability within hierarchies of authority.
3. Often, there is pressure to move on to a new project before the current one has been operating long enough to be observed carefully. This promotes a sense of being accountable only for meeting schedules.
4. The contagion of malpractice suits currently afflicting the medical profession is carrying over into engineering. With this comes a crippling preoccupation with legalities, a preoccupation makes one wary of becoming morally involved in matters beyond one's strictly defined institutional role.

We do not mean to underestimate the very real difficulties these conditions pose for engineers who seek to act as morally accountable people on their jobs. Much less do we wish to say engineers are blameworthy for all the harmful side effects of the projects they work on, even though they partially cause those effects blameworthiness, and also to confuse causal responsibility with moral responsibility. But we do claim that engineers who endorse the perspective of engineering as a social experiment will find it more difficult to divorce themselves psychologically from personal responsibility for their work. Such an attitude will deepen their awareness of how engineers daily cooperate in a risky enterprise in which they exercise their personal expertise toward goals they are especially qualified to attain, and for which they are also accountable.

3.8 ROLE OF CODES

Inspiration and guidance. Codes provide a positive stimulus for ethical conduct and helpful guidance concerning the main obligations of engineers. Often, they succeed in inspiring by using language with positive overtones. Since codes should be brief to be effective, they offer mostly general guidance. More specific directions may be given in supplementary statements or guidelines, which tell how to apply the code. Further, specificity may also be attained by the interpretation of codes.

Support codes. Give positive support to those seeking to act ethically. A publicly proclaimed code allows an engineer who is under pressure to act unethically to say, "I am bound by the code of ethics of my profession".

Deterrence and discipline codes. They can also serve as the formal basis for investigating unethical conduct. Where such investigation is possible, a motive for not acting immorally is provided as a deterrent. Such an investigation generally requires paralegal proceedings designed to get at the truth about a given charge without violating the personal rights of those being investigated.

In the past, engineering professional societies have been reluctant to undertake such proceedings because they have lacked the appropriate sanctions needed for punishment of misconduct.

Educational and mutual understanding. Codes can be used in the class room and elsewhere to prompt discussion and reflection on moral issues and to encourage a shared understanding among professionals, the public, and government organizations concerning the moral responsibilities of engineers. They can help do this because they are widely circulated and officially approved by professional societies.

Contributing to the profession's public image. Codes can present a positive image to the public of an ethically committed profession. Where the image is warranted, it can help engineers more effectively serve the public. It can also win greater powers of self regulation for the profession itself, while lessening the demand for more government regulation. Where unwarranted, it reduces to a kind of window dressing that ultimately increases public cynicism about the profession.

Protecting the status quo. Codes establish ethical conventions which can help promote an agreed upon minimum level of ethical conduct. But they can also stifle dissent with the profession. On occasions a code has positively discouraged moral conduct and caused serious harm to those seeking to serve the public.

Promoting business interests. Codes can place unwarranted self serving items that can take on great undue influence. Obviously, there is disagreement about which, if any, entries function in these ways. Some engineers believe that in the past the codes were justified in forbidding competitive bidding, while others agree with the decision of the Supreme Court in the case of the *National Society of Professional Engineers* vs. *the United States* (April 25, 1978) that such a restriction is inappropriate.

3.9 CODES AND EXPERIMENTAL NATURE OF ENGINEERING

The perspective of engineering as social experimentation provides some help in deciding which functions should be primary in engineering codes. It clearly emphasizes those that best enable concerned engineers to express their views freely—especially about safety—to those affected by engineering projects. Only thus can clients and the public be educated adequately enough to make informed decisions about such projects. Contemporary working conditions within large corporations do not always encourage this freedom of speech. In such a situation, a code of ethics can provide an important counter-balance. Thus the supportive function seems to be of primary importance.

Chapter 4

Engineers' Responsibility for Safety and Risk

We demand safe products and services because we do not wish to be threatened by potential harm, but we also realize that we may have to pay for this safety. To complicate matters, what may be safe enough for one person may not be so for someone else either because of different perceptions about what is safe or because of different predispositions to harm. For example, a power saw in the hands of a child will never be as safe as it can be in the hands of an adult. And a sick adult is more prone to suffer ill effects from air pollution than is a healthy adult. Absolute safety, in the sense of a degree of safety that satisfies all individuals as groups under all conditions, is neither attainable nor affordable.

4.1 SAFETY AND RISK

Paradoxical though it may seem, safety is both a very precise and a vague term. It is vague because, to some extent, safety is a vague judgement, but precise because in many cases, we can readily distinguish a safe design from an unsafe one. Risk is a key element in any engineering design. It is impossible to design anything to be completely risk free. How much risk is appropriate? How safe is safe enough?

4.1.1 Concept of Safety

"A thing is safe if its risks are judged to be acceptable". This approach helps underscore the notion that judgements about safety are tacitly value judgements about what is acceptable risk to a given person or group. Differences in appraisals of safety are thus correctly seen as reflecting differences in values. This can be shown if we consider three types of situations that can arise. Imagine, first, a case where we seriously underestimate the risks of something, say of using a toaster we see at a garage sale. On the basis of that mistaken view, we judge it to be very safe and buy it. On taking it home and trying to make toast with it, however, it sends us to the hospital with a severe electric shock and burn. Using the ordinary notion of safety, we conclude we were wrong in our earlier judgement. The toaster was not safe at all. Given our values and our needs, its risks should not have been judged acceptable earlier. Consider the second case where we grossly overestimate the risks of something. For example, we irrationally think fluoride in drinking water will kill a third of the populace. It would, however, be impossible for someone to prove that the water is actually safe. The water became unsafe the moment we judged the risks of using it to be unacceptable for us.

4.2 TYPES OF RISKS

The dictionary defines risk as the possibility of suffering harm or loss. Risk is sometimes used synonymously with danger. It also defines safety as freedom from damage, injury, or risk. We engage in risk behaviour when we do something that is unsafe, and something is unsafe if it involves substantial risk. Although these definitions are precise, safety and risk are essentially subjective and depend on many factors:

4.2.1 Voluntary vs. Involuntary Risk

Many consider something safer if they knowingly take the risk, but would find it unsafe if forced to do so. If the property values are low enough, some people will be tempted to buy a house near a plant that emits low levels of a toxic waste into the air. They are willing to assume the risk for the benefit of cheap housing. However, if a person already living near a plant finds that toxic fumes are emitted by the plant and he was not informed, the risk will appear to be larger, since it was not voluntarily assumed.

4.2.2 Short-term vs. Long-term Consequences

Something that might cause a short-lived illness or disability seems safer than something that will result in permanent disability. An activity for which there is a risk of getting a fractured leg will appear much less risky than an activity with a risk of a spinal fracture since a broken leg will be painful and disabling for a few months, but generally full recovery is the norm. Spinal fractures, however, can lead to permanent disability.

4.2.3 Expected Probability

Many persons might find a 1 in 1,000,000 chances of a severe injury of any kind to be an acceptable risk, whereas a 50-50 chance of a somewhat minor injury might be unacceptable. Swimming at a beach where there is known to be a large concentration of jellyfish would be unacceptable to many since there would be a high probability of a painful though rarely fatal sting. Yet, at the same beach, the risk of a shark attack is low enough that it does not deter anyone from swimming, even though such an attack would very likely lead to death or dismemberment. It is important to remember here that the expected probability is only a reversible effect. Something will seem less risky if the bad effects are ultimately reversible. This concept is similar to the short-term vs. long-term risk.

4.2.4 Reversible Effects

Something will seem less risky if the bad effects are ultimately reversible. This concept is similar to the short-term vs. long-term risk.

4.2.5 Threshold Levels for Risk

Something that is risky only at fairy high exposures will seem safer than something with a uniform exposure to risk. For example, the probability of being in an automobile accident is the same regardless of how often you drive). You can reduce the likelihood of being in an accident by driving less often). In contrast, studies have shown that low levels of nuclear radiation actually have beneficial effects on human health while only at higher levels of exposure do death or severe health problems occur. If there is a threshold for the effects, generally there will be a greater tolerance of risk.

4.2.6 Delayed vs. Immediate Risk

An activity whose harm is delayed for many years will seem much less risky than something with an immediate effect. For example, for several years now, Americans have been warned about the adverse long-term health effects of a high-fat diet. This type of diet can lead to chronic heart problems or stroke later in life. Yet, many ignored these warnings and are unconcerned about a risk that is so far in the future. These same people might find an activity such as skydiving unacceptably risky since an accident will cause immediate injury or death.

Thus, whether something is unsafe or risky often depends on the type of person. Something that one person feels safe may seem very unsafe to someone else. This creates some confusion for the engineer who has to decide whether a project is safe enough to be pursued. Ultimately, it is up to the engineer and company management to use their professional judgement to determine whether a project can be safely implemented.

4.3 SAFETY AND THE ENGINEER

Since safety is an essential aspect of our duties as engineers, how can we be sure that our designs are safe? There are four criteria that must be met to help ensure a safe design. *First*, the minimum requirement is that a design must comply with the applicable laws. This requirement should be easy to meet since legal standards for product safety are generally well known, are published, and are easily accessible. *Second*, an acceptable design must meet the standard of "accepted engineering practice". You cannot create a design that is less safe than what everyone else in the profession understands to be acceptable. To address this issue, an engineer must continually upgrade her skills by attending conferences and short courses, discussing issues with other engineers, and constantly surveying the literature and trade magazines for information on the current state of the art in the field. *Third*, alternative designs that are potentially safer must be explored. This requirement is also difficult to meet since it requires a fair amount of creativity in seeking alternative solutions. This creativity can involve discussing design strategies with others in your field and brainstorming new alternatives with them. The best way to know if your design is the safest available is to compare it with other potential designs. *Finally*, the engineer must attempt to foresee potential misuses of the product by the consumer and must design to avoid these problems. Again, this requires a fair amount of creativity and research. It is always tempting to think that if someone is stupid enough to misuse your product, then it is their own fault and the misuse and its consequences should not bother you too much. However, an engineer should execute designs in such a way as to protect even someone who misuses the product. Of course, a court is not always concerned with the stupidity of the user and may pass severe strictures and impose heavy penalty against you if it feels that a product was not properly designed. Placing a warning label on products is not sufficient and is not a substitute for doing the extra engineering work required to produce a safe design.

4.4 DESIGNING FOR SAFETY

How should safety be incorporated into the engineering design process?

1. *Define the problem.* This step includes determining the needs and requirements and often involves determining the constraints.
2. *Generate several solutions.* Multiple alternative designs are created.
3. *Analyze each solution to determine the pros and cons of each.* This step involves determining the consequences of each design solution and determining whether it solves the problem.
4. *Test the solutions.*
5. *Select the best solution.*
6. *Implement the chosen solution.*

In step 1, it is appropriate to include issues of safety in the product definition and specification. During steps 2 through 5, engineers typically consider issues of how well the solution meets the specifications, how easy it will be to build, and how costly it will be. Safety is especially important in step 5, where the engineer attempts to assess all of the trade-offs required to obtain a successful final design. In assessing these trade-offs, it is important to remember that safety considerations should be paramount and should have relatively higher weight than other issues.

Minimizing risk is often easier said than done. There are many things that make this a difficult task for the engineer. For example, the design engineer often must deal in uncertainties. Many of the risks can only be expressed as probabilities and are no more than educated guesses. Sometimes, there are synergistic effects between probabilities, especially in a new and innovative design for which the interaction of risks will be unknown. Are minimizing risks and designing for safety always the more expensive alternatives? Spending a long time in engineering a safer product may seem like a very expensive alternative, especially early in the design cycle before the product has been built or is on the market. This, however, is a very short-term view. The prudent and ethical thing to do is to spend as much time and money as possible up front to engineer the design correctly so as to minimize future risk of injury and subsequent criminal or civil actions against you.

4.5 Risk-Benefit Analysis

One method, which engineers sometimes use to help analyze risk and to determine whether a project should proceed, is called *risk-benefit analysis*. This technique is similar to the cost-benefit analysis. In risk-benefit analysis, the risks and benefits of a project are assigned dollar amounts, and the most favourable ratio between risks and benefits is sought. Recall that cost-benefit analysis is tricky because it is frequently difficult to assign realistic dollar amounts to alternatives. This task is especially difficult in risk-benefit analysis because risks are much harder to quantify and more difficult to put a realistic price tag on. Still, this can be a useful technique if used as part of a broader analysis and only if used objectively. In doing a risk-benefit analysis, one must consider who takes the risks and who reaps the benefits. It is important to be sure that those who are taking the risks are also those who are benefiting. This consideration is fundamental to issues of economic justice in our society and can be illustrated by the concept of "environmental racism", which is the placing of hazardous-waste sites, factories with unpleasant or noxious emissions, etc. near the least economically advantaged neighbourhoods. The only ethical way to implement risk-benefit analysis is for the engineer to ensure to the greatest extent possible that the risks as well as the benefits of his design are shared equally in society.

4.6 ACCIDENTS

There are many ways in which accidents can be categorized and studied. One method is to group accidents into three types: procedural, engineered, and systemic. *Procedural accidents* are perhaps the most common and are the result of someone making a bad choice or not following established procedures. For example, in the airline industry, procedural accidents are frequently labelled as "pilot error". These are accidents caused by the misreading of an important gauge, flying when the weather should have dictated otherwise, or failure to follow regulations and procedures. In the airline industry, this type of error is not restricted to the pilot; it can also be committed by air-traffic controllers and maintenance personnel.

Engineers must also guard against procedural problems that can lead to accidents. These problems can include failure to adequately examine drawings before signing off on them, failure to follow design according to accepted engineering practice. Procedural accidents are fairly well understood and are amenable to solution through increased training, more supervision, new laws or regulations, and closer scrutiny by regulations.

Engineered accidents are caused by flaws in the design. These are failures of material devices that do not perform as expected, or devices that do not perform well under all circumstances. For example, microcracks sometimes develop in turbine blades in aircraft engines. When these cracks become severe enough, the blade can fail and break apart. Sometimes, this has resulted in penetration of the cabin by metal fragments, causing injury to passengers. Engineered failures should be anticipated in the design stage and should be caught and corrected during testing. However, it is not always possible to anticipate every condition that will be encountered, and sometimes testing doesn't occur over the entire range of possible operating conditions. These types of accidents can be understood and reduced as more knowledge is gained through testing and actual experience in the field.

Systemic accidents are harder to understand and harder to control. They are characteristic of very complex technologies and the complex organizations that are required to operate them. A perfect example of this phenomenon is the airline industry. Modern aircrafts are complicated systems. Running them properly requires the work of many individuals, including baggage handlers, mechanics, flight attendants, pilots, government regulators and inspectors, and air-traffic controllers. At many stages in the operation of airline, there are chances for mistakes to occur, some with serious consequences. Often, a single, minor mistake is not significant, but a series of minor mistakes can add up to a disaster. The airline industry is not the only complex engineered system in our society that is susceptible to systemic accidents. Both modern military systems, especially nuclear weapons, for which complicated detection and communication systems are relied on for control, and nuclear power plants with complicated control and safety systems, have documented failures in the past that can be attributed to this type of systemic problem. The Bhopal gas tragedy is a classic case of systemic accident.

What are the implications of this type of accident for the design engineer? Because it is difficult to take systemic accidents into account during design, especially since there are so many small and seemingly insignificant factors that come into play, it may seem that the engineer bears no responsibility for this type of accident. However, it is important for the engineer to understand the complexity of the systems that he is working on and attempt to be creative in determining how things can be designed to avert as many mistakes as possible by people using the technology. As designers, engineers are also partially responsible for generating owner's manuals and procedures for the use of the devices they design. Although an engineer has no way of ensuring that the procedures will be followed, it is important that he be thorough and careful so that the accident could be averted.

Chapter 5

Responsibilities and Rights

Loyalty and collegiality are essential aspects of team work in engineering. Collegiality is an important virtue even though it may seem to be out of place when there is competition among engineers from different companies. The central elements of collegiality are respect, commitment, connectedness, and cooperation. *Respect* is affirming the worth of other engineers engaged in producing socially useful and safe products. *Commitment* means sharing a devotion to the moral ideal inherent in the practice of engineering. *Connectedness* is an awareness of being part of a cooperative undertaking created by shared commitments and expertise.

5.1 COLLEGIALITY

Collegiality is an amorphous concept and refers to an environment characterized by professionalism, a general sense of well-being, and a spirit of cooperation. There is no formula for becoming collegial or maintaining collegiality and, to a large extent, collegiality is a consequence of pursuing sound approaches.

5.1.1 Techniques for Achieving Collegiality

Some of the techniques are now described.

(i) Development recognition and articulation of shared values. In many firms, one can identify a handful of partners who are central to the collegiality of the organization. The attitudes and shared values of these partners become critically important to maintaining the desired environment. Does the firm have leaders who represent a model of performance? Does the leadership of the firm talk about firm's values other than money? If the firm is really just about the business of maximizing income for its partners, how can it expect to retain the loyalty of its partners if it has a bad year or if there are opportunities in the market place for its partners to make more money? If the ties that bind are only economic, the organization will be highly unstable and vulnerable. Most unstable environments sooner or later become decidedly non-collegial and partners in such organizations frequently become disrespectful of each other.

(ii) Establishing/restoring a sense of professionalism. Leadership of a firm can restore a sense of professionalism regarding client service and the role of the lawyer in the resolution of disputes, the conduct of business, and the overall order of our society. How lawyers in the firm behave towards one another, the staff of the firm, their own clients, adversary counsel, the courts, government officials and the public at large, matter greatly in establishing a culture of compatibility. Good behaviour reflecting civility, courtesy, respect, fair dealing and honesty cannot be legislated, but high standards should be established as part of what it means to be a lawyer in the firm. Simply put, lawyers who cannot behave in a professional manner destroy collegiality.

(iii) Vision. An organizational vision or mission is important to a sense of well-being, and is the essence of a sense of purpose. A firm's vision could well be "we want to remain a twenty lawyer firm practicing in insurance defense work in X area". A firm in which there is no agreed purpose, or dramatically different visions of the firm in constant unresolvable tension, can easily become uncollegial.

(iv) Defining expectations. Discord within a firm frequently arises because of disappointment at unfulfilled expectations. Frequently, the expectations which become disappointments are also uncommunicated in the first instance. Without undue rigidity, it is important to establish and articulate the criterion of what it means to be a partner in your firm. What overall time commitment is expected? What general billable hour commitment is expected? What time commitment for business development is expected? Whether there is a minimum expectation for all partners, or whether there are tailored expectations, is less important than having communications about and agreements over the general expectations. A criterion is also important in regulating the selection of partners laterally or from the associate ranks. An example of a criterion would be: a partner in the law firm is expected to make a strong contribution in at least three of the four areas—business origination, management of work, production, and firm administration or community service. Expectations should also be defined for associates on a firm commitment basis. Collegiality within the associate ranks is directly affected by the billable hour requirements for the associates. The firm should carefully consider the impacts of billable hour requirements for associates. By setting very high billable hour requirements, the firm risks creating an atmosphere of exploitation and may greatly limit the overall development of associates.

(v) Paying attention to structure. Managing expectations is a key to a collegial environment. Some firms are utilizing contract arrangements (e.g. senior counsel, contract attorney, or contract partner) to slot lawyers in arrangements where there is a base salary plus a bonus tied to performance. These arrangements may permit a firm to retain a valuable lawyer who has been trained by the firm, without diluting or overexpanding the partnership. These contractual arrangements, if fairly administered, can be used to permit greater flexibility in life style choices by lawyers.

(vi) Paying attention to gender and diversity issues. Collegiality can be enhanced or diminished by whether and how the leadership of the firm deals with issues of gender and diversity. Is the firm really committed to equal opportunity hiring? Are opportunities within the firm really fairly open without regard to race and gender? Openness and a commitment to fairness is important in establishing a collegial environment. Moreover, a firm which has women and minorities in important positions will have significant advantages in attracting business.

(vii) Score-keeping. How the firm defines and determines productivity can contribute to, or be destructive of, a collegial environment. Lawyers tend to be remarkably attuned to "score-keeping" issues. If a firm gave "billable hour" credit for jogging, most of its lawyers would probably be in good shape, or break down with bad knees. It is easy to measure some aspects of productivity, such as collections on a lawyer's time in straight billable hour cases. Other aspects of productivity, such as business development or effectiveness in managing work, may be more difficult to measure. Many questions should be considered. Should the firm track business development effort and success? Should the tracking be numeric or on some other basis (e.g. narratives in year end compensation memos)? If the firm does not track business development efforts, how will it be able to reward this aspect of performance? How does the firm handle billing? Is the partner managing the case handling the billing functions, or is the billing function retained by the lawyer who originated or controls the client? How does the firm's approach in these areas affect the way work is handled? Is the environment one in which work is passed on to the lawyer best able to handle the matter, or is work being hoarded? Does the firm consist of individual lawyers who are in reality competing with each other, or does it consist of lawyers acting as a team, each trying to maximize firm profitability and trying to provide the best service possible to the client? Firms, as a general rule, should stimulate external efforts to develop business, and internal efforts to refer work within the firm to the best lawyer. There should be accountability for good case management; in many instances the discontent between the billing attorney and the attorney managing the case prevents effective accountability. Score-keeping practices frequently evolve in response to the demands by strong partners and should be examined periodically. At the very least, the score-keeping practices should be clearly articulated and understood, and should at least be open for discussion.

(viii) Compensation. There are two distinct aspects of compensation which impact on collegiality: one is the profitability of the firm and the other is how profits are distributed. If a firm cannot achieve reasonable profitability on a per partner basis, great pressure is placed on the distribution process. Management's role is not only to encourage the steps that produce reasonable profitability, but also to manage expectations so that they will be in line with profitability. A compensation system should (a) motivate partners to perform in ways that maximize firm profits and to cause the firm to achieve its other objectives; (b) reward performance and contribution; and (c) solidify the ties with partners who are critical to the ongoing success of the institution.

Fairness, as an abstract concept, is probably less important than rewarding (keeping happy) those partners who are vital to the preservation and success of the venture. Within certain ranges, relative compensation may be more important than actual compensation. How a partner is compensated vis-à-vis another contemporary, or someone who is perceived to be at the same "level", can easily affect morale. Differences in compensation among partners should seem generally reasonable and explainable with reference to the values of the firm. Procedural fairness may be as important as the substantive criteria used for compensation. Assuming some measure of subjectivity in the system, it is very important that partners believe there has been thoughtful consideration of their contribution and views regarding compensation. It is extremely important that a partner be able to effect changes in his or her compensation by changes in performance, and that these changes can occur over a reasonably short time span of, say, two or three years.

Among the most difficult issues in compensation are:

1. To what extent should compensation in the current year be tied to current year performance, or be determined by a share of profits based on historic contribution?
2. How does the firm address the compensation demands of its superstars?
3. How quickly does the firm respond to the compensation demands of its younger partners as they become extremely productive and start to acquire substantial business?
4. How does the firm value hard work versus business generation.

Rational compensation systems vary significantly in addressing each of these issues. For the organization to be collegial and stable, those partners with the economic horsepower to threaten or destroy the firm must view the firm as insiders with a proprietary interest, and not as claimants seeking to extract as much as possible from the organization. Firms confronted by a claimant mentality tend to try appeasement which is frequently unsatisfying to the claimant and others in the organization. (We use "appeasement" to reflect what Churchill described as feeding the crocodile in the hope that it would eat you last.)

(ix) Trust. The vast majority of partners in law firms are hard working, ethical, competent and honest. There should be an atmosphere of trust among partners and between the management of the firm and its partners. The necessity of rules and procedures should be carefully examined, and there should be a distinct bias against controls on partner behaviour. Communicated expectations are more effective generally than proscriptions. In a milieu of trust, however, there must be the capacity to sanction behaviour amounting to a lack of trust. Moreover, a trusting firm does not have to be a firm which is "sleep walking." However, it must have the capability to identify and deal with those partners who are not worthy of trust.

(x) Practice area leadership. Although there are many loners who have been very successful in practicing law, the complexity of issues, the need for specialized expertise, and the work demands of the profession generate significant pressure to utilize practice groups in day to day law firm operations. How these groups are led is extremely important to the success of the firm, and to the general sense of well being among its participants. At one extreme is a model in which practice groups have virtually no organizational standing or role; at the other is where firms treat practice groups as separate profit centres. There is no right or wrong approach, and the effectiveness of practice areas is more dependent on actual leadership rather than organization chart responsibilities. If the firm utilizes practice areas, there should be articulated expectations.

(xi) Selection process. Compatibility factors, including whether the individual is a team player, should be considered in virtually every decision involving lawyers of new associates, in decisions to make associates partners, in the decision to make non-equity partners equity partners, and in the selection of leaders of the firm. The focus on compatibility can assuredly be overdone and many organizations can accommodate difficult personalities. However, if the firm values collegiality, it seems basic and sensible to consider whether individuals being brought into the firm as lawyers are considerate of others, respect others, treat subordinates fairly and with dignity, are thoughtful and caring, and are capable of unselfish behaviour. It is difficult to imagine a collegial organization of abusive, selfish, egocentric, greedy and neurotically self-indulgent people.

(xii) Helpfulness. Firms in which lawyers are effectively "enemies competing against one another" for business and recognition, tend to be unhappy. Firms in which the lawyers are out to help each other, tend to be happy and productive. An expectation of helpfulness is important. Recognition of helpfulness by firm management through compensation and other forms of recognition is extremely important. Punishing behaviour which is antithetical to helpfulness is extremely important.

(xiii) Balance of power. On the theory that power corrupts and absolute power corrupts absolutely, law firms should consciously seek balances of economic power within the firm. It is healthier to have a firm built on many sources of business generation, rather than on one or a few. It may be beneficial to have balance among practice areas, and balance between or among offices in a multioffice environment. Branch offices frequently fail because the management in the "home" office is essentially indifferent to the professional fates of those in a distant service office. A "single firm" concept is important to overcoming unbalanced economic power among practice groups or offices.

(xiv) Partner evaluations. Critical self analysis, done in a constructive and positive spirit, can be useful and affirming. Partner evaluations can be used to deliver otherwise hard to deliver messages, and to communicate praise and appreciation; they can also serve as a legitimate channel by the law firm's leadership to receive information, complaint and suggestion. Not all firms need the formality or structure of partner evaluations. Firms which neither have evaluations nor open communications of the type which would occur in evaluations, risk smouldering unhappiness and may lack the information to know what is going wrong.

(xv) Problem partners. The firm's approach to dealing with problem partners is highly relevant to its overall collegiality, and to its values. Some firms can be unmerciful in culling the herd. Those firms tend to be driven to maximize profits, and everyone gets the message that his or her value to the firm is dependent on continuous high performance. Such environments tend to produce significant profits and lot of stress; loyalty of partners to the firm may be diminished owing to diminished loyalty of the firm to the partners. Other firms consciously decide not to act quickly to give the partner a real chance, or they simply lack the will to deal with problem partners. In these firms, the problem partners hang around, draining valuable money through compensation and cause productive partners to snipe (and sometimes even to leave). These firms tend to emphasize values other than profitability and a culture of caring. It is demoralizing where leadership of the firm lacks capacity to act. It is an expression of a moral value if the leadership, having the capacity to act, chooses not to, out of considerations of fairness or because of a reasonable belief that the partner can be productive. In an environment in which one or more partners are not flourishing, the collegiality of the firm is adversely affected if the approach of leadership is simply to let such partners twist in wind. Expectations should be communicated; teaming arrangements can be suggested to explore whether the partner can become productive. Either an overly aggressive or passive approach in dealing with problem partners harms the collegiality of the organization. The issues with associates are not dissimilar, except that there are different expectations and perhaps different capacities to change.

(xvi) Business development. An important technique in establishing and maintaining a collegial environment is to have team marketing focusing on particular industries or clients.

5.2 TWO SENSES OF LOYALTY

Loyalty to an employer can mean two things. Agency-loyalty is acting to fulfil one's contractual duties to an employer. These duties are specified in terms of the particular tasks for which one is paid, as well as the more general activities of cooperating with colleagues and following legitimate authority within the corporation. As its name implies, agency-loyalty is entirely a matter of actions, whatever its motives. Identification-loyalty, by contrast, has as much to do with attitudes, emotions, and a sense of personal identity as it does with actions. It can be understood as agency-loyalty that is motivated by identification with the group to which one is loyal. It implies seeking to meet one's moral duties to a group or organization willingly, with personal attachment and affirmation". People who detest their employers and companies, who do their work grudgingly or spitefully, are not loyal in this sense, even though they may adequately perform all their work responsibilities and hence manifest agency-loyalty.

In both these senses, loyalty can be a desirable character attribute. Either sense might be meant when codes of ethics assert that engineers ought to be loyal to employers, or that they should act as their employer's or client's faithful agents or trustees'. Certainly, there are specific duties intended, such as those specified by subheadings under the injection to be a faithful agent or trustee; to avoid conflicts of interest, to inform employers of any possible conflicts of interest, to protect confidential information, to be honest in making estimates, to admit one's errors, and so on.

5.2.1 Obligations of Loyalty

Loyalty based on personal identification is obligatory when two conditions are met. First, employees must see some of their own important goals as met by and through a group in which they participate. Typically, these goals include the pleasures of affiliating with the group, recognition from the group that one's contributions are valuable, and a sense of worth and accomplishment in pursuing the goals of the group. Second, employees must be treated fairly, each receiving (roughly) his or her share of benefits and burdens. Once these conditions are met, employees acquire obligations to identify with groups and sometimes to support groups in particular ways.

5.2.2 Misguided Loyalty

Both agency and identification loyalty can be shown toward corporations as a whole or toward smaller divisions within corporations. For example, an engineer might identify closely with a group of committed professionals while working on a particular project, but might identify less with the more impersonal vast conglomerate comprising a large international firm. Conversely, an engineer might identify with the corporation but not with a particular team to which he is assigned. Sometimes, inappropriate or misguided loyalty to a project team or supervisor can harm corporations, as well as the general public.

5.2.3 Professionalism and Loyalty

There are three points about the relationship between professional responsibility and loyalty to companies or employers. *First*, acting on professional commitments to the public can be a more effective way to serve a company than a mere willingness to follow company orders. *Second,* it is clear from the example that loyalty to companies or their current owners should not be equated with merely obeying one's immediate supervisor. *Third*, an engineer may have professional obligations to both an employer and to the public, which reinforce rather than contradict each other. Thus, there need be no general contrast between the moral status of employees and professionals, In fact, obligations to the public and to one's employer often point in the same direction. Sometimes, an engineer seeking to protect the public is overruled by top management for financial reasons. At other times there are disagreements over technical matters, and engineers are told they must not push their own views further.

5.3 PROFESSIONAL RIGHTS

Engineers also have rights that go along with these responsibilities. Not all of these rights come about due to the professional status of engineering. There are rights that individuals have regardless of professional status, including the right to privacy, the right to participate in activities of one's own choosing outside of work, the right to reasonably object to company policies without fear of retribution, and the right to due process. The most fundamental right of an engineer is the right of professional conscience. This involves the right to exercise professional judgement in discharging one's duties and to exercise this judgement in an ethical manner. This right is basic to an engineer's professional practice. However, it is no surprise that this right is not always easy for an employer to understand. The right of professional conscience can have many aspects. For example, one of these aspects may be referred to as the "Right of Conscientious Refusal". This is the right to refuse to engage in unethical behaviour.

But quite simply, no employer can ask or pressurize an employee into doing something that he considers unethical and unacceptable. Although this issue is very clear in cases for which an engineer is asked to falsify a test result or fudge on the safety of a product, it is less clear in cases for which the engineer refuses an assignment based on an ethical principle that is not shared by everyone. For example, an engineer ought to be allowed to refuse to work on defense projects or environmentally hazardous work if his conscience says that such work is immoral. Employers should be reasonably accommodating of such requests.

5.4 PROFESSIONAL RESPONSIBLITIES

We will begin our discussion of professional rights and responsibilities by first looking more closely at a few of the important responsibilities that engineers have.

5.4.1 Confidential and Proprietary Information

A hallmark of the professions is the requirement that the professional keeps certain information of the client secret or confidential. Confidentiality is mentioned in most engineering codes of ethics. This is a well-established principle in professions such as medicine, where the patient's medical information must be kept confidential, and in law, where "councel-client privilege" is a well-established doctrine. This requirement applies equally well to engineers, who have an obligation to keep proprietary information of their employer or client confidential.

Why must some engineering information be kept confidential? Most information about how a business is run, its products and its suppliers, directly affects the company's ability to compete in the marketplace. Such information can be used by a competitor to gain advantage or to catch up. Thus, it is in the company's (and the employee's) best interest to keep such information confidential to the extent possible. What types of information should be kept confidential? Some of these types are very obvious, including test results and data, information about upcoming unreleased products, and designs or formulas for products. Other information that should be kept confidential is not as obvious, including business information such as the number of employees working on a project, the identity of suppliers, marketing strategies, production costs, and production yields. Most companies have strict policies regarding the disclosure of business information and require that all employees sign such disclosure forms. Frequently, internal company communications will be labelled as "proprietary". Engineers working for a client are frequently required to sign a nondisclosure agreement. Of course, those engineers working for the government, especially in the defense industry, have even more stringent requirements about secrecy placed on them and may even require a security clearance granted after investigation by a governmental security agency before being able to work. It seems fairly straightforward for engineers to keep information confidential, since it is usually obvious what should be kept confidential and from whom it should be kept. However, as in many of the topics that we discuss in the context of engineering ethics, there are gray areas that must be considered. For example, a common problem is the question of how long confidentiality extends after an engineer leaves employment with a company. Legally, an engineer is required to keep information confidential even after he has moved to a new employer in the same technical area. In practice, doing so can be difficult. Even if no specific information is divulged to a new employer, an engineer takes with him a great deal of knowledge of what works, what materials to choose, and what components not to choose. This information might be considered proprietary by his former employer. However, in a new job, an engineer cannot be expected to forget all of the knowledge already gained during years of professional experience. The courts have considered this issue and have attempted to strike a balance between the competing needs and rights of the individual and the company. Individuals have the right to seek career advancement wherever they choose, even for a competitor of his current employer. Companies have the right to keep information away from their competitors. The burden of ensuring that both of these competing interests are recognized and maintained lies with the individual engineer.

5.5 CONFLICT OF INTEREST

Professional conflicts of interest are situations where professionals have an interest which if pursued might keep them from meeting their obligation to their employers or clients. Sometimes, such an interest involves serving in some other professional role, say, as a consultant for a competitor's company. Other times it is a more personal interest such as making substantial private investment in a competitor's company. This threat to meeting professional obligations makes it clear why conflicts of interest have been given prominence in engineering, codes of ethics in management policy statements, and in law.

5.5.1 Solving Conflict Problems

Conflict problems can be solved in three ways. Often, there are conflicting moral choices, but one is obviously more significant than the other. For example, protecting the health and safety of the public is more important than your duty to your employer. In this type of case, the resolution of the conflict involves an easy choice. A second solution is an attempt at some kind of a compromise that will work for everyone. The emphasis here should be on the word "creative" because it takes a great deal of creativity to find a middle ground that is acceptable to everyone and a great deal of diplomacy to sell it to everyone. Finally, when there is no easy choice and attempts to find a middle ground are not successful, all that is left is to make the hard choice. Frequently, you must rely on "gut feelings" for which path is the correct one.

Concern about conflicts of interest largely centres on their potential to distort good judgement, especially where professionals are involved. Exercising good judgement means arriving at beliefs on the basis of expertise and experience as opposed to merely following simple rules. Conflicts of interest threaten good judgement in faithfully serving an employer or client. Thus we can refine our definition of conflicts of interest by saying that they typically arise when two conditions are met: 1. The professional is in a relationship or role that requires exercising good judgement on behalf of the interest of an employer or client. 2. The professional has some additional or side interest that could threaten good judgement in serving the interests of the employer or client.

Being in a conflict of interest is not merely being confronted with conflicting interest. A student, for example, may have interests in excelling on four final exams. She knows, however, there is time to study adequately for only three of them and so she must choose which interest not to pursue. Or an investor may strongly desire to invest in two stocks but have sufficient funds for investment in only one. In these cases "conflicting interests" means a person has two or more desires that cannot all be satisfied given the circumstances. But there is no suggestion that it is morally wrong or problematic to try pursuing them all. By contrast, in professional conflict of interest, it is often physically or economically possible to pursue all the conflicting interests but it is morally problematic whether one should do so. Conflict of interest can arise in innumerable ways and with many degrees of subtlety. In each case the general test for identifying conflicts of interest is whether there is any possibility of an outside interest influencing one's judgement or the judgement of typical professional in serving clients or employers.

Avoiding conflict of interest is important in any profession, and engineering is no exception. A conflict of interest arises when an interest, if pursued, could keep a professional from meeting one of his obligations. For example, a civil engineer working for a state department of highways might have a financial interest in a company, that has a bid on a construction project. If that engineer has some responsibility for determining which company's bid to accept, then there is a clear conflict of interest.

5.6 SELF-INTEREST, CUSTOMS AND RELIGION

Moral reasons and ideals form a distinct category of value different from other category of values. Let us make this clearer by relating and contrasting moral values to three other types of values—self-interest, customs, and religion.

5.6.1 Ethical Egoism

Each of the major ethical theories recognizes the importance of self-interest. Utilitarians take into account one's own good as well as the good of others. Duty ethicists emphasize duties to ourselves including the duty to respect ourselves and care prudently for our own well-being. Rights ethicists accept our rights to pursue our own good. And virtue ethicists (as well as duty ethicists) emphasizes the importance of self-respect, which implies looking after one's own needs.

At the same time, each of these theories insists that the pursuit of self-interest must be balanced and restrained by moral responsibilities to other people. Let us consider a view that challenges all these theories, a view that tries to reduce morality to the pursuit of self-interest. The view is called ethical egoism: "ethical" because it is a theory about morality, and "egoism" because it says that the sole duty of each of us is to maximize his or her own good.

Defenders of ethical egoism draw a distinction between narrower and wider forms of self interest. To be selfishly preoccupied with one's own private good to the point of indifference and disregard for the good of others will cut one off from rewarding friendship and love. Hence the 'paradox of happiness'. Personal well-being generally requires some wider interest in others although the rational egoist insists that the only reason for showing an interest in others is for the sake of oneself.

There is a problem with this last claim, however, Friendship and love seem to require caring for other people at least in part for themselves. Not merely from ulterior motives of self concern. They require valuing other people for their sake, and not solely because they serve one's personal ends.

What about business and professional life? Ethical egoists try to defend the position by contending that an ironic consequence of everyone rationally pursuing their self interest is that everyone benefits. For example, the classical economists Adam Smith and his contemporary defender Milton Friedman believe that society benefits most when (a) individuals pursue their private good; and (b) corporations (as expressions of many individual wills) pursue maximum profits in a competitive free market. The idea is that this will make economy prosper, thereby benefiting everyone because each individual and organization is in the best position to know what is good for them and for how best to pursue that good.

The requirements of morality and prudence point in the same direction. Indeed, professional life would be unbearable unless, for the most part, the human notice of self interest and moral concern did not point in roughly the same direction. Thus the prudent employee and the morally conscientious engineer for the most part look alike in their conduct, but only for the most part. Morality require a willingness on the part of both individuals and corporations to place some restraints on the pursuit of private interests.

5.7 COLLECTIVE BARGAINING

Is it possible for engineers to be professionals, dedicated to the highest ethical standards of professional conduct, and loyal to their companies while simultaneously being members and supporters of a union? The question is too complex to allow a simple answer. Before answering it, we need to know what kind of union and union activities are at issue. Lacking this information, a definitive answer is not possible. Many observers have argued that the ethical aspects of professionalism in engineering are inherently unionism— that is, with union ideology and practice. A number of professional societies have also held that loyalty to employers and the public is incompatible, and inconsistent with any form of collective bargaining.

5.8 CONFIDENTIALITY

Keeping confidence is one of the most central and widely acknowledged duties of any professional. Defense lawyers must keep clients' information confidential, doctors and counsellors must keep information on their patients confidential, and teachers must keep at least personal information about their students confidential. Confidential information is information deemed desirable to be kept as secret. "Keep Secret" is a relational expression. It always makes sense to ask, "Secret with respect to whom?" In the case of some government organizations, such as the CBI (India) FBI and CIA (USA), highly elaborate systems for classifying information have been developed that identify which individuals and groups may have access to what information. Within other governmental agencies and private companies, engineers and other employees are usually expected to withhold information labelled "confidential" from unauthorized people, both inside and outside the organization. Most business tacitly adopt yet another criterion; Confidential information is any information that the employer or client would like to have kept secret in order to compete effectively against business rivals. Often this is understood to be any data concerning the company's business or technical processes that are not already public knowledge. While this criterion is somewhat vague, it clearly points to the employer or client as the main source of the decision as to what information is to be treated as confidential.

5.9 ACCEPTANCE OF BRIBES/GIFTS

One of the many grey areas of engineering ethics is the acceptance of gifts from vendors or the offering of gifts to customers to secure business. The difficulty here comes because of the potential for gifts to become bribes or to be perceived as bribes. Frequently, engineers find themselves in the position of either dealing with vendors who wish to sell them products for incorporation into the engineer's work or acting as vendors themselves and working on sales to other engineers or companies. By definition, a bribe is something, such as money or a favour, offered or given to someone in a position of trust in order to induce him to act dishonestly. It is something offered or serving to influence or persuade. What are the ethical reasons for not tolerating bribery? *First*, bribery corrupts our free-market economic system and is anticompetitive. Unlike the practice of buying the best product at the best price, bribery does not reward the most efficient producer. One can argue the virtues or vices of the free-market economy, but it is the system under which our economy operates, and anything that subverts this system is unfair and unethical. *Second*, bribery is a sellout to the rich. Bribery corrupts justice and public policy by allowing rich people to make all the rules. In business, it guarantees that only large, powerful corporations will survive since they are more capable of providing bribes. A small start-up company doesn't have the resources to compete in an environment where expensive favours are required to secure business. *Finally*, bribery treats people as commodities that can be bought and sold. This practice is degrading to us as human beings and corrupts both the buyer and the seller.

5.9.1 When is a Gift a Bribe?

Frequently, the boundary between a legitimate gift and a bribe is very subtle. Gifts of nominal value, such as coffee mugs or calendars with a vendor's logo and phone number on it, are really just an advertising tool. Generally, there is no problem with accepting these types of items. Dining with a customer or a supplier is also an acceptable practice, especially if everyone pays his or her own way. It is important from the point of view of both suppliers and customers that good relations be maintained so that good service can be provided. Social interaction, such as eating together, often facilitates the type of close and successful interactions required by both sides. However, when meals or gifts are costly, and their expenses are not equally shared, the possibility for abuse becomes large.

5.9.2 Examples of Gifts vs. Bribes

To help illustrate the differences between bribes and legitimate gifts, let us look at a few potential scenarios to see how fuzzy this boundary can be:

- During a sales visit, a sales representative offers you a coffee mug with his company's name and logo on it. The value of the mug is Rs. 250. Can you accept this item? Does the answer to this question change if this item is, say, Rs. 10,000 crystal bowl with the name of the company engraved on it? How about if there is no engraving on it?
- Your meeting with a sales representative is running into the lunch hour. He invites you to go out for lunch. You go to fast-food restaurant and pay for your own lunch. Is this practice acceptable? Does the answer to this change if you go to an expensive five star hotel and if he pays for the lunch?
- A sales representative from whom you often purchase asks if you would like to play tennis with him this weekend at one of the local municipal courts. Should you go? Is the answer to this question different if the match is at an exclusive local club to which he belongs? What if he pays the club's guest fee for you?
- A company sales representative would like you to attend a one-day-sales seminar in Bangalore (you are stationed in New Delhi). Your company will pay for your trip. Should you go? What if the sales representative's company is going to pay for you to go? What if your family is invited as well?

Keep in mind that gifts accepted even after the purchase of something from a company might be a bribe directed at securing future sales from you or might be aimed at engineers at other companies. Although nothing was said about a gift up front, now that you have received one, the expectation of gifts might affect your future purchase decisions. Similarly, an employee of a company like yours might become aware of the gift that you received. He now realizes that if he orders parts from the same supplier that you did, he will receive a gift similar to yours. He will be tempted to order from this supplier even if there is a better supplier of that product in the market. These types of gifts tend to shut out smaller companies that can't necessarily afford gifts and might also cause an increase in everyone's costs since, if everyone now expects to receive gifts, the product cost will go up. Clearly, bribery is pernicious, and even the appearance of bribery should be avoided as the saying goes, Caesar's wife must not only be above board but must be seen to be above board.

5.9.3 Problem Solving

Bribery can easily be analyzed by looking at the factual, conceptual, and moral issues described previously. Frequently, the facts will be obvious: who offered a gift, what its value was, and what its purpose was. Conceptual issues will be somewhat more difficult since it must be determined whether the gift is of sufficient value to influence a decision or whether that influence is the intent of the gift. Once the conceptual issues have been worked out and it is clear whether or not the gift is a bribe, the moral issue is often very clear.

A bribe is a substantial amount of money or goods offered beyond a stated business contract with the aim of winning advantage in gaining or keeping the contract. "Substantial" is a vague term but it alludes to amounts, beyond acceptable gratuities, that are sufficient to distort the judgement of a typical person. Typically, though not always, bribes are made in secret. Gifts are not bribes as long as they are small gratuity offered in the normal conduct of business. Prearranged payments made by contractors to companies or their representatives if they exceed the amount for contracts actually granted, are called "kickbacks". When suggested by the granting party to the party bidding the contract, the latter often defends its participation in such an arrangement as having been subjected to "extortion".

Often companies offer gifts to selected employees of government agencies or partners in trade. Many such gifts are unobjectionable; some are intended as bribes and still others create conflicts of interest that do not, strictly speaking, involve bribe. What are the differences? In theory, these distinctions may seem clear but, in practice, they become blurred. Bribes are illegal or immoral because they are substantial enough to threaten fairness in competitive situations, while gratuities are of smaller amount. Some gratuity play a legitimate role in the normal conduct of business which others can bias judgement like a bribe does. Much depends on the context that there are numerous gray areas, which is why companies often develop elaborate guidelines for their employees.

Company policies generally ban any gratuity that have more than nominal value or any realistic potential for biasing judgement. In part, the specific criteria for nominal value will be what is widely and openly accepted as normal business practice. In part, it will be assessed by a person's own awareness of what might influence his or her judgement. And in part, it must be weighed according to how others might perceive (or misperceive) the gratuity as influencing the judgement of a typical professional in that situation.

Employed engineers are more likely to be the objects of bribery attempts than to be the initiators. But once they occupy management roles or operate their own companies, the pressures of meeting completion date or satisfying the bottom line frequently lead to moral lapses—violations of the "moral bottom line".

5.9.4 Interests in Other Companies

Some conflicts of interest consist in having an interest in a competitor's or a subcontractor's business. One glaring example is actually working for the competitor or subcontractor as an employee or consultant. Another example is partial ownership or substantial stock holdings in the competitor's business. Does holding a few shares of stock in a company one has occasional dealings with constitute a conflict of interest? Usually not, but as the number of shares of stock increases, the issue becomes blurry. Again, is there a conflict of interest if one's spouse works for a subcontractor to one's company? Usually not, but a conflict of interest arises if one's job involves granting contracts to that subcontractor.

5.10 OCCUPATIONAL CRIMES

Occupational crimes are illegal acts made possible through one's lawful employment (as opposed to say, the illegal "work" of the "professional" bank robber). It is the secretive violation of laws regulating work activities. When committed by office workers or professionals, occupational crime is called "white-collar crime". Many occupational crimes are special instances of conflicts of interest, especially when the crime involves personal gains or leads to failure to meet professional obligations.

Occupational crime can take other forms including crimes that are aimed at promoting the interests of one's employer rather than oneself. Moreover, occupational crime deserves greater attention because of the frequency and magnitude as also due to the increasing public attention paid to it. Employee theft is a type of occupational crime when it is associated with an employee's assigned tasks.

Examples of occupational crimes include employee crime, white collar crime, embezzlement and fraud, computer theft and trade secrets.

Employee crime. It involves:

1. The employees who manage their own businesses making use of their employer's resources.
2. The store managers who steal items from incoming shipments and sell the goods.
3. The trusted employees selling company products illegally and pocketing the proceeds.

White collar crime. White collar crimes take place mostly at the workplaces and involve activities related to otherwise legitimate occupations. Theft by white collar employees ranges from taking office supplies for personal use to the theft of products intended for sale. At the highest level, the white collar crime typically involves manipulation of accounting records or legal documents for personal gain. Other variations of white collar crimes abound. Another example is insider trading that allows dealers in shares to use information before others know of it to make an illicit profit from their trading activities.

Embezzlement and fraud. Embezzlement and fraud is committed by either commission or omission. An act of commission involves lying or making some form of material misrepresentation, whereas an act of omission refers to any failure to disclose a significant fact that the law requires to be disclosed.

Computer theft. Unless authorized explicitly, misuse of computers is unethical. The employee who examines, uses, or copies information or programs contained in a data bank might leave the original information or programs unchanged (the company might never even realize what the employee did). Nevertheless, such unauthorized use constitutes theft.

Trade secrets. Trade secrets are concerned with a company's own activities, technologies, and future plans. These secrets, if known to competitors, would materially affect the company's ability to compete commercially against these competitors. The company does not want anyone outside the company to have that information. For example, a company which develops a secret process to manufacture high density computer diskettes may take explicit measures to protect that process as a trade secret. Similarly, lists of suppliers or customers, research results, computer programs, marketing and production plans can all constitute trade secrets. However, skills that an employee acquires by working for a company do not count as trade secrets because trade secrets consist of information and not skills. The misuse of proprietary information has become alarming as new "information technologies" have increasingly turned information into a valuable asset to which employees have regular access.

5.10.1 Industrial Espionage

The term *espionage* means spying or counter-intelligence. To cite an example, a major centre for development and manufacture of integrated circuit microprocessors or computer chips has attracted vast numbers of creative engineers. It has also attracted industrial espionage on a massive scale. The reasons are several. Innovation is so rapid that products become often outdated within two years. Fortunes can be made or lost depending on how quickly new products are developed and marketed. Computer chips can be extremely expensive to develop. Dismantling a competitor's device and reconstructing the same to produce an identical product that can be offered at a lower price is possible (development costs are nonexistent). Employees who betray company secrets may smuggle trade secrets from one company and sell them to others; thus provide criminal "expertise".

5.10.2 Price Fixing

The Sherman Antitrust Act (1890, USA), which prohibits companies from jointly fixing prices in ways that restrain free competition and trade, has frequently been violated in the electrical equipment industry, where large contracts and few competitors are the norm (Oligopoly). Top officials of Westinghouse, General Electric, and other manufacturers were indicted for conspiring to fix prices of large electrical apparatus. A number of defendants did not view their activities as criminal or harmful, even though they knew they were 'technically' illegal. In fact, many of them defended their conduct as beneficial to society as it stabilizes the prices. The practice of price fixing had been so rampant in the industry for so long that it is now accepted as proper.

5.10.3 Endangering Lives

Occupational hazards are to be clearly informed to the employees. Law allows the employees to gain compensation (beyond workers' compensation) without having to prove that a crime has been committed. This is true even when people die as a result of horrendous corporate negligence. For instance, take the case of Manville Corporation (formerly Johns–Manville Corporation)—the largest producer of asbestos. Asbestos fibres in the lungs cause asbestosis (a debilitating lung disease) and mesothelioma (an incurable cancer). However, Manville Corporation concealed this information from the workers and the public who had a right to be asked for informed consent to the dangers confronting them. When the company was finally brought to trial, the company officials claimed that many of their company's own studies of asbestos had mysteriously disappeared from their files. Asbestos-related diseases can develop after only two to three months of exposure. More than 100,000 people have already died due to asbestos-related diseases.

5.11 WHISTLE BLOWING

Whistle blowing is the act by an employee of informing the public or higher management of unethical or illegal behaviour by an employer or supervisor. There are frequent newspaper reports of cases in which an employee of a company has gone to the media with allegations of wrong doing by his employer or in which a government employee has disclosed waste or fraud. Whistle blowing is the act of reporting on unethical conduct within an organization to someone outside of the organization in an effort to discourage the organization from continuing the activity. In the usual case, the charges are made by an employee or former employee who has been unable to obtain the attention of the organization's management to the problem. Sometimes, whistle blowing is confined to within the organization where the whistle blower's supervisor is bypassed in an appeal to higher management. An important issue is to determine the conditions under which engineers are justified in blowing the whistle. It is morally permissible for engineers to engage in whistle blowing when the following conditions are met:

1. The harm that will be done by the product to the public is considerable and serious.
2. Concerns have been made known to the superiors and got no satisfaction from their immediate superiors, all channels have been exhausted within the corporation including the board of directors.
3. The whistle blowers must have documented evidence that would convince the reasonable, impartial observer that his or her view of the situation is correct and the company position is wrong.
4. There must be strong evidence that releasing the information to the public would prevent the projected serious harm.

Clearly, a person engaging in whistle blowing runs considerable risk of being labelled a malcontent or of being charged with disloyalty and possibly being dismissed. The decision to blow the whistle requires great moral courage. Some far sighted companies have established the office of ombudsman (e.g. Times of India) or an ethics review committee to head off and solve these problems internally before they reach the whistle blowing stage.

5.11.1 Type of Whistle Blowing

Internal whistle blowing occurs when an employee goes over the head of an immediate supervisor to report a problem to a higher level management. Or, all levels of management are bypassed, and the employee goes directly to the president of the company or the board of directors. It is kept within the organization. External whistle blowing occurs when the employee goes outside the company and reports wrongdoing to newspapers or law-enforcement authorities. Either type of whistle blowing is likely to be perceived as disloyalty. However, keeping it within the company is often seen as less serious than going outside of the company. Anonymous whistle blowing occurs when the employee who is blowing the whistle refuses to divulge his name when making accusations. These accusations might take the form of anonymous memos to upper management or anonymous phone calls to the police. The employee might also talk to the news media but refuses to let her name be used as the source of the allegations. Acknowledged whistle blowing, on the other hand, occurs when the employee puts his name behind the accusations and is willing to whistle blowing the scrutiny brought on by his accusations. Whistle blowing can be very bad from a corporation's point of view because it can lead to distrust, disharmony, and an inability of employees to work together.

5.11.2 When should Whistle Blowing be Attempted?

Whistle blowing should only be attempted if the following four conditions are met.

Need. There must be a clear and great harm that can be avoided by blowing whistle. In deciding whether to go public, the employee needs to have a sense of proportion. For example, if an accident occurs at your company, resulting in a spill of a small quantity of a toxic compound into a nearby waterway that is immediately cleaned up, this incident probably does not merit notifying outside authorities. However, if this type of event happens repeatedly and no action is taken to rectify the problem despite repeated attempts by employees to get the problem fixed, then perhaps this situation is serious enough to warrant the extreme measures of whistle blowing.

Proximity. The whistle blower must be in a very clear position to report on the problem. Hearsay is not adequate. First-hand knowledge is essential to making an effective case about wrongdoing. This point also implies that the whistle blower must have enough expertise in the area to make a realistic assessment of the situation. The condition stems from the clauses in several codes of ethics that mandate an engineer not to undertake work in areas outside his expertise. This principle applies equally well to making assessments about whether wrongdoing is taking place.

Capability. The whistle blower must have a reasonable chance of success in stopping the harmful activity. You are not obligated to risk your career and the financial security of your family, if you can't see the case through to completion or you don't feel that you have access to the proper channels to ensure that the situation is resolved.

Last resort. Whistle blowing should be attempted only if there is no one else more capable or more proximate to blow the whistle and if you feel that all other lines of actions within the context of the organization have been explored and shut off. A great deal of introspection and reflection is required before whistle blowing is undertaken.

5.11.3 Preventing Whistle Blowing

Even organizations with a very strong ethical culture will have employees who, from time to time, succumb to the temptation to do something wrong. A typical corporate approach to stemming whistle blowing and the resulting bad publicity is to fire whistle blowers and to intimidate others that might seem likely to blow the whistle. This type of approach is both ineffective and ethically unacceptable. No one should be made to feel bad about trying to stop ethically questionable activities.

There are four ways to solve the whistle blowing problem within a corporation. *First*, there must be a strong corporate ethics culture. This should include a clear commitment to ethical behaviour, starting at the highest levels of management and mandatory ethics training for all employees. All managers must set the tone for the ethical behaviour of their employees. *Second*, there should be clear lines of communication within the corporation. This openness gives an employee a clear opportunity to express his concerns as he feels there is something serious that must be remedied. *Third*, all employees must have meaningful access to high-level managers in order to bring their concerns forward. This access must come with a guarantee that there will be no retaliation. Rather, employees willing to come forward should be rewarded for their commitment to fostering the ethical behaviour of the company. *Finally*, there should be willingness on the part of management to admit mistakes, publicly if necessary. This attitude will set the stage for ethical behaviour by all employees.

Chapter 6

Global Issues

We live in an age when technical and political changes have been taking place more rapidly than at any time in the past. The scale and range of societies, the size of projects undertaken by them—projects concerned with education, health care, government, public works and many other areas of common concern—have greatly increased over those undertaken in previous centuries. Perhaps the rate of change is even more significant than the scale of change. In addition to the scale and rate of change, and the changes in population distribution, we have to recognize the nature of the change. Technological developments have placed vastly increased sources of power under the direction of mankind and have very much enhanced the speed with which we can communicate with one another. Within decades the time taken to communicate with some parts of the world has been reduced from months to seconds.

6.1 GLOBALIZATION

In parallel with this development there has been an unprecedented increase in the population in the developing countries, requiring quite different social relationships and dependencies than has been the case in the past. Each of these factors affects our traditional values. The behaviour of men and women in authority is a reflection of the values and behaviour of the societies in which they operate.

Until the second half of the 20th century, most organizations operated within circles that shared their cultural and social structure—often a single cultural framework. Operations outside this sphere were seldom directly influenced by the different cultures or the values encountered. Indeed, other value systems were not generally considered or even observed. As a result, companies and nations became or remained ‘closed’.

In the recent past, technology and media expansion have 'shrunk' the world and society, reinforcing the concept of all people having common concerns, and needing to reconcile differences in their value systems. These changes in outlook have been reflected in significant international high-level discussions driven by the recognition of common concerns of all national communities. In recent years there have been global summits on topics such as:

The Environment, 1992
Human Rights, 1993
Population, 1994
Social Development, 1995
Women, 1996.

These summits have provided a mechanism by which the aggravating effects of shrinking resources, sustainability and expanding demand can also be addressed.

The globalization of markets has been accompanied by the development and growth of multinational corporations (MNCs) which operate across local and national boundaries. These businesses have become international, or indeed supranational, more rapidly than many of the national communities in which they operate and they have influenced the nature of the development cycle by their presence. The increasing international flows of capital, technology, trade and people have had the effect of changing the nature of local organizations, governments and people of countries, and have led to social changes and development.

The influences and effects of global enterprise and competition on exporting and/or host countries can be far-reaching. It is important that respect for cross-cultural differences and concern for human as well as business interests is developed and maintained. It cannot always be assumed that we know what they want and what is good for them. Mutually acceptable aims, values and standards are vital if economic success and public acceptance are to be assured.

6.2 CROSS-CULTURAL ISSUES

World communities are much more interdependent. Differing views as to the nature of the 'good and of the 'right' have a real impact on peace and prosperity. The decisions of a single powerful individual can affect the lives of many millions of others for better or for worse. The issues arising from this globalization are complex. They require an in-depth study of the value systems and the physical, economic, political and cultural parameters of all the individuals and communities involved. This requires a cross-cultural ethical audit of a much more strategic nature than the audit of a particular project or enterprise. The professional engineer may have neither the training nor the experience to carry out such a study. It may, however, be within his authority to ensure that all these factors are considered, and to engage the assistance of fellow professionals who can make an objective and understanding assessment of the situation. The operations under consideration may involve a high degree of risk. They may be subject to fluctuations in the money markets, or instability and disturbance in some of the nations involved. Local limitations may make it difficult to carry out some of the tasks. There may be no local legislation to control contractual relationships or health and safety aspects of the work, as well as monitor environmental impact.

One of the most rewarding aspects of the engineering profession is the enabling of activities that improve the quality of the lives of others, without diminishing the rich variety of human experience and fulfillment. The need to identify the factors that may become conflicts of interest within traditional value systems is an ethical responsibility of the professional. Preventing conflicts prove valuable in reducing delays, in accommodating changes of design and construction practice, and in ensuring collaborative working between people of differing cultural and experiential backgrounds. But being transnational, it is likely to lie beyond the reach of national laws and professional codes; individual self-regulation is again of prime importance.

Responding to ethical dilemmas in the engineering context cannot always be straightforward, not least because life itself is rarely so. Hence, handling such dilemmas requires:

- Ethical thinking that enables the professional to understand the data, values and consequences of the case.
- Careful attention to methods so that the dilemma is not turned into a crusade—social and self-awareness and the development of a professional value system.
- Awareness and development of codes of ethics, in particular companies, or on a particular project, so that ethical discussions are open and evident
- Awareness and development of interdisciplinary codes and cross-cultural factors.

Because no simple rules will deal with all ethical problems, the exercise of responsibility becomes central. This involves establishing the responsibilities to the several parties concerned, which requires negotiation, to ensure that the professional does not take on too much responsibility. The professional must, however, take responsibility for ethical dilemmas and work through the ethical decision-making process, avoiding any denial of responsibility. Such responsibilities cannot be confined to particular roles. The responsibilities of the engineer and the engineering profession include those to society in general.

6.3 ENVIRONMENTAL ETHICS

One of the most important political issues of the late 20th century has been environmental protection and the rise of the environmental movement. This movement has sought to control the introduction of toxic and unnatural substances into the environment, to protect the integrity of the biosphere, and to ensure a healthy environment for humans. Engineers are responsible in part for the creation of the technology that has led to damage of the environment and are also working to find solutions to the problems caused by modern technology. The environmental movement has led to an increased awareness among engineers that they have a responsibility to use their knowledge and skills to help protect the environment. As concern about the environment has grown, ethicists have turned their attention to the ethical dimensions of environmentalism. In the late 1960s, an area of study called "environmental ethics" was formulated, seeking to explore the ethical roots of the environmental movement and to understand what ethics tells us about our responsibility to the environment.

Fundamental to discussing ethical issues in environmentalism is a determination of the moral standing of the environment. Our Western ethical tradition is *anthropocentric*, meaning that only human beings have moral standing. Animals and plants are important only in respect of their usefulness to humans. This type of thinking is often evident even within the environmental movement when a case is sometimes made for the protection of rare plants based on their potential for providing new medicines. If animals, trees, and other components of the environment have no moral standing, then we have no ethical obligations towards them beyond maintaining their usefulness to humans. There are, however, other ways to view the moral standing of the environment.

One way to explore the environment's moral status is to try to answer some questions regarding the place of humans in our environment. Do we belong to nature, or does nature belong to us? If animals can suffer and feel pain like humans, should they have moral standing? If animals have moral standing, how far does this moral standing then extend to other like forms, such as trees? Clearly, these questions are not easily answered, and not everyone will come to the same conclusion. However, there are significant number of people who feel that the environment, and specifically animals and plants, do have standing beyond their usefulness to humans. In one form, this view holds that humans are just one component of the environment and that all components have equal standing. For those who hold this view, it is an utmost duty of everyone to do what is required to maintain a healthy biosphere for its own sake.

Regardless of the goal (i.e., either protecting human health or protecting the overall health of the biosphere for its own sake), there are multiple approaches that can be taken to resolving environmental problems. The first approach is sometimes referred to as the *cost-oblivious approach.* In this approach, cost is not taken into account, but rather the environment is made as clean as possible. No level of environmental degradation is seen as acceptable. This approach bears a striking resemblance to rights and duty ethics. There are obvious problems with this approach. It is difficult to uphold, especially in modern urbanized society. It is very difficult to enforce, since the definition of "as clean as possible" is hard to agree on, and being oblivious to cost is not practical in any realistic situation, in which there are not infinite resources to apply to a problem.

A second approach is based on *cost-benefit analysis*, which is derived from utilitarianism. Here, the problem is analyzed in terms of the benefits derived by reducing the pollution. Improvements in human health, for example, and the costs required to solve the problem. The costs and benefits are weighed to determine the optimum combination. In this approach, the goal is not to achieve a completely clean environment, but rather to achieve an economically beneficial balance of pollution with health or environmental considerations.

There are problems associated with the cost-benefit approach. *First*, there is an implicit assumption in cost-benefit analysis that cost is an important issue. But what is the true cost of a human life or the loss of a species or a scenic view? These values are difficult, if not impossible, to determine. *Second*, it is difficult to accurately assess costs and benefits, and much guesswork must go into these calculations. *Third*, this approach does not necessarily take into account who shoulders the costs and who gets the benefits. This is frequently a problem with the sitting of landfills and other waste dumps. The cheapest land is in economically disadvantaged areas, where people do not necessarily have the political clout, education, or money required to successively oppose a landfill in their neighbourhood. Although dumps have to go somewhere, there should be some attempt to share the costs as well as share the benefits of an environmentally questionable project. *Finally*, cost-benefit analysis does not necessarily take morality or ethics into account. The only considerations are costs and benefits, with no room for a discussion of whether what is being done is right or not.

Given the complexity of these issues, what then are the responsibilities of the engineer to the environment? When looking at the environmental aspects of his work, an engineer can appeal to both professional and personal ethics to make a decision. Of course, the minimal requirement is that the engineer must follow the applicable central, state, and municipal laws and regulations.

Professional codes of ethics tell us to hold the safety of people and the environment to be of paramount importance. So, clearly, engineers have a responsibility to ensure that their work is conducted in the most environmentally safe manner possible. This is true certainly from the perspective of human health, but for those who feel that the environment has moral standing of its own, the responsibility to protect the environment is clear. Often, this responsibility must be balanced somewhat by consideration of the economic well-being of our employer, our family, and our community.

Our personal ethics can also be used to determine the best course when we are confronted with an environmental problem. Most of us have very strong beliefs about the need to protect the environment. Although these beliefs may come into conflict with our employer's desires, we have the right and duty to strongly express our views on what is acceptable. As professionals, engineers have the right to express their opinions on moral issues such as the environment. An engineer should not be compelled by his employer to work on a project that he finds ethically troubling, including projects with severe environmental impacts.

In trying to decide what the most environmentally acceptable course of action is. It is also important to remember that a basic tenet of professional engineering codes of ethics states that an engineer should not make decisions in areas in which he is not competent. For many environmental issues, engineers are not competent to make decisions, but should instead seek the counsel of others such as biologists, public-health experts, and physicians who have the knowledge to help analyze and understand the possible environmental consequences of a project.

6.4 COMPUTER ETHICS

Computers have rapidly become a ubiquitous tool in engineering and business. There are ways in which computers have benefits to society. Unfortunately, there are also numerous ways in which computers have been misused, leading to serious ethical issues. The engineer's roles as designer, manager, and user of computers bring with them a responsibility to help foster the ethical use of computers.

Many ethical problems associated with computer use relate to unauthorized use of information stored on computer databases and are thus related to the issues of confidentiality and proprietary information. The ethical problem-solving techniques will be equally applicable to computer ethics issues.

There are three broad categories of computer ethics problems: those for which the computer is the instrument of the unethical act, such as the use of a computer to defraud a bank; those for which the computer is the object of the act, as when computer software is stolen and installed on one's own computer or when information is accessed from someone else's computer; and those problems associated with the autonomous nature of computers.

6.4.1 Computers as the Instrument of Unethical Behaviour

Many uses are merely extensions to computers of other types of unethical acts. For example, computers can be used to more efficiently steal money from a bank. A more traditional bank-robbery method is to put on a mask, hand a note to a bank teller, show your gun, and walk away with some cash. Computers can be used to make bank robbery cashier to perform and hard to trace. The robber simply sits at a computer terminal, perhaps the modern equivalent of a mask invades the bank's computer system, and directs that some of the bank's assets be placed in a location accessible to him. Using a computer, a criminal can also make it difficult for the theft to be detected and traced.

It is clear that from an ethical standpoint, there is no difference between a bank robbery perpetrated in person or one perpetrated via a computer, although generally the amounts taken in a computer crime far exceed those taken in an armed robbery. The difference between these two types of robbery is that the use of the computer makes the crime impersonal. The criminal never comes face to face with the victim. In addition, the use of computer makes it easier to steal from a wide variety of people. Computers can be used to steal from an employer, outsiders can get into a system and steal from an institution such as bank, or a company can use the computer to steal from its clients and customers. In these cases, the computer has only made the theft easier to perpetrate, but does not alter the ethical issues involved. Unfortunately, the technology to detect and prevent this type of crime greatly lags behind the computer technology available to commit it. Those seeking to limit computer crime are always playing a catch-up game.

Another instrumental area of computer ethics involves *privacy*. It is widely held that certain information is private and cannot be divulged without consent. This includes information about individuals as well as corporate information. Computers did not create the issues involved in privacy, but they certainly have exacerbated them. Computers make privacy more difficult to protect since large amounts of data on individuals and corporations are centrally stored on computers where an increasing number of individuals can access it. Before we look at the ways that privacy can be abused by the use of computers, we will discuss the issues surrounding privacy and see what the ethical standing or privacy is.

By privacy, we mean the basic right of an individual to control access to and use of information about himself. Why is privacy an ethical issue? Invasions of privacy can be harmful to an individual in two ways. *First*, the leaking of private information can lead to an individual's being harassed or blackmailed. In its most simple form, this harassment may come in the form of repeated phone calls from telemarketers who have obtained information about an individual's spending habits. The harassment might also come in the form of subtle teasing or bothering from a co-worker who has gained personal knowledge of the individual. Clearly, individuals have the right not to be subjected to this type of harassment. *Second*, personal information can also be considered personal property. As such, any unauthorized use of this information is theft. The same principle applies to proprietary information of a corporation.

How do computers increase the problems with privacy protection? This phenomenon is most easily seen by looking at the old system of record keeping. For example, medical records of individuals were at one time kept only on paper and generally resided with the individual's physician and in hospitals where a patient had been treated. Access to those records by researchers, insurance companies, or healthcare institutions was a somewhat laborious process that involved searching through storage for the appropriate files, copying them, and sending them through the mail. Unauthorized use of this information involve breaking into the office where the files were kept and stealing them or, for those who had access to the files, surreptitiously removing the files. Both these acts meant a substantial risk of being caught and prosecuted. In some hospitals, these records have now been computerized. Although computerization makes the retrieval of files much easier for those with legitimate needs and reduces the space required to store the files, it also makes the unauthorized use of this information by others easier.

6.4.2 Computers as the Object of Unethical Acts

Ethical issues also arise when computers are the objects of an unethical act. This act is popularly referred to as *hacking* and has been widely reported in the newspapers and in popular culture, sometimes with the "hacker" being portrayed as heroic. Hacking comes in many forms: gaining unauthorized access to a database, implanting false information in a database or altering existing information, and disseminating viruses over the Internet. These activities are by no means limited to highly trained computer specialists. Many hackers are bored teenagers seeking a challenge. Computer hacking is clearly ethically troublesome. As mentioned before, accessing private information violates the privacy rights of individuals or corporations even if the hacker keeps this information to himself. In extreme cases, hackers have accessed secret military information, which has obvious implications for national security. Altering information in a database, even information about yourself, is also ethically wrong.

The issuance of computer viruses is also unethical. These viruses frequently destroy data stored on computer. In extreme cases, this act could lead to deaths when hospital records or equipment are compromised to financial run for individuals whose records are wiped out or even to the loss of million of dollars for corporations, individuals, and taxpayers, as completed work must be redone after being destroyed by a virus. Hackers are not being malicious, but are simply trying to "push the envelope" and see what they and their computers are capable of. Nevertheless, hacking is an unethical use of computers.

6.4.3 Autonomous Computers

Other ethical concerns arise because of the increasingly autonomous nature of computers. Autonomy refers to the ability of a computer to make decisions without the intervention of humans. Some of the negative implications of this autonomy are chillingly spelled out in 2001: "A space odyssey", by Arthur C. Clarke, in which an autonomous computer responsible for running a spaceship headed for Jupiter begins to turn against the humans it was designed to work for. Certainly, there are applications for which autonomy is valuable. For example, manufacturing processes that require monitoring and control at frequent intervals can greatly benefit from autonomous computers. In this case, the autonomy of the computer has very little impact beyond the interests of the manufacturer.

Computers are widely used to automate trading on the major stock exchanges. Some brokerages and institutional investors utilized computers that were programmed to sell stocks automatically under certain conditions, among them when prices drop sharply. This type of programming creates an unstable situation. As prices drop, computers automatically start selling stocks, further depressing the prices, causing other computers to sell, and so on until there is a major market crash.

This scenario actually occurred on October 19, 1987, when the Dow Jones Industrial Average (a widely used market-price indicator) dropped by 508 points, a 22.6 per cent drop in the overall value of the market. Interestingly, during the famous October 1929 stock market crash that launched the Great Depression, the drop in overall market value was only half of this amount. The 1987 crash was widely attributed to help prevent a recurrence of this problem.

Autonomy of computer systems has also been called into question with regard to military weapons. Many weapons systems rely heavily on computer sensors and computer controls. Due to the speed with which events can happen on a modern battlefield, it would seem valuable to have weapons that can operate autonomously. However, weapons systems operating without human intervention can suffer from the instability problems described with regard to the financial markets. For example, a malfunctioning sensor might lead a computer to think that an enemy has increased its military activity in a certain area. This would lead to an increased readiness on our part, followed by increased activity by the enemy, etc. Thus, unstable situation could lead to a conflict and the loss of life when really there was nothing happening. This problem is especially disconcerting due to the implications of loss of human life. It is clear from this example that although autonomous computers can greatly increase productivity and efficiency in many areas, ultimately there must be some human control in order to prevent disasters.

6.4.4 Computer Codes of Ethics

To help decision making regarding these and other computer-related ethics issues, many organizations have developed codes of ethics for computer use. Codes are guidelines for the ethical use of computing resources, but should not be used as a substitute for sound moral reasoning and judgement. They do, however, provide some guidance in the proper use of computer equipment.

6.5 WEAPONS DEVELOPMENT

One of the largest employers of engineers worldwide is the defense industry. This is by no means a modern trend; throughout history, many innovations in engineering and science have come about as a result of the development of weapons. Since weapons are designed besically for one purpose—to kill human beings—it is important to look at this type of engineering work in the context of engineering ethics and the rights of engineers. An engineer may choose either to work or not to work in defense-related industries and be ethically justified in either position. Many reasonable engineering professionals feel that, ethically, they cannot work on designs that will ultimately be used to kill other humans. Their remoteness from the killing site does not change this feeling. Even though they will not push the button, trigger the gun or may never actually see the victims of the weapon, they still find it morally unacceptable to work on such systems.

On the other hand, equally morally responsible engineers find this type of work ethically acceptable. They reason that the defense of our nation or other nations from aggression is a legitimate function of our government and is an honourable goal for engineers to contribute to. Both these positions can be justified by reference to the moral theories and problem-solving techniques. Even if an engineer finds defense work ethically acceptable, there might be uses of these weapons or certain projects that he considers questionable. For example, is it acceptable to work on weapons systems that will only be sold to other nations, particularly to those engaged in conflicts? Is the use of weapons to guarantee our "national interests," such as maintaining a steady supply of foreign oil, an acceptable defense project?

Given the issues that surround defense work, what is an engineer to do when asked to work on a weapons project he considers questionable? As with many of the ethical dilemmas, there is no simple solution, but rather the answers must be determined by each individual after examination of his values and personal feelings about the ethics of defense work. It is important to avoid working on any project that you deem unethical, even if it might lead to a career advancement, or even if it is a temporary job. This principle also holds true for projects that you feel are unsafe, dangerous for the environment, etc. It can be argued that weapons work is the most important type of engineering, given its consequences for mankind. Because of the implications to human life, this type of engineering requires an even more stringent examination of ethical issues to ensure responsible participation.

6.6 ETHICS AND RESEARCH

There are two major ethical issues related to research: honesty in approaching the research problem and honesty in reporting the results. The first relates to a state of mind essential to successfully performing research. This state of mind includes avoiding preconceived notions about what the results will be, being open to changing the hypothesis when such action is warranted by the evidence, and generally ensuring that an objective frame of mind is maintained.

Results must also be accurately reported. Once an experiment or test has been performed, the results of the experiment must not be overstated, but rather an accurate assessment and interpretation of the data must be given. The environment that most researchers work in India do not foster innovation rewards or research results. Academic researchers must publish significant research results in order to get tenure at their universities. If an experiment is not working out, it is tempting to "massage" the results to achieve the desired outcome. Even for researchers in industrial environments or faculty who are already tenured, the quest for fame or the desire to be the first with new results can be overwhelming and can lead to falsification of data. Often, the pressure to get a new product to market leads the test engineer to "fudge" data to qualify the product.

It is important to note the distinctions between intentional deception and results or interpretations that are simply incorrect. Sometimes, results are published that, upon further research, turn out to be incorrect. This situation is not an ethical issue unless a clarification of the results is presented. Rather, this issue indicates that great care must be taken before results are initially reported.

It is also important to ensure that proper credit is given to everyone who participated in a research project. Rarely is research performed by a single investigator working alone in his laboratory. Generally, there is participation by other people, who should be acknowledged for their contributions such as discussions or guidance, construction of experimental apparatus, or substantial help with performing experiments or interpreting data.

It is tempting to think that fraud and deception in research are rare and only perpetrated by lower level scientists, but this perception is decidedly untrue. There are many examples of well-known and even Nobel prize-winning scientists who have had lapses of ethical judgement with respect to their research. For example, Robert Millikan was a physicist from the University of Chicago who won the 1923 Nobel Prize in Physics for experiments that measured the electrical charge of the electron. Studies of Millikan's unpublished data indicate that he excluded 49 of the 140 experimental observations from the paper that he published. However, in the paper, he stated that the published work contained all of the data. Inclusion of this data would not have changed his conclusions, but would have made the result seem more certain and the experiment more clearly definitive.

6.7 ANALYSING ETHICAL PROBLEMS IN RESEARCH

How can ethical issues relating to research be best analyzed? Perhaps, the easiest means to determine what is best ethically in performing research and experiment is to consult the codes of ethics of the engineering professional societies. All these codes include language requiring engineers to be honest in reporting the results of work and assigning credit for the work done. For example, the code of all American Institute of Chemical Engineers states that "members shall... treat fairy all colleagues and co-workers, recognize the contributions of others...,"and "issue statements and present information only in an objective and truthful manner." These statements apply equally well to all professional activities of an engineer, including research, experiment, and testing.

The ethical theories can also be used to analyze issues involving research. Utilitarianism or rights and duty ethics can be applied to research, but it is perhaps easiest to examine research issues using virtue ethics. One of the virtues is honesty. Honesty facilitates trust and good relations between individuals, whereas dishonesty leads to doubts and misgivings about others. People rarely want to associate with those who they feel do not behave fairly and cannot be trusted. Making false claims about the results of experiments is certainly a form of dishonesty. Likewise, not giving credit to everyone who has participated in a project is dishonest, and virtue ethics maintains that this practice is unacceptable.

6.8 INTELLECTUAL PROPERTY RIGHTS (IPRs)

Intellectual Property is a class of property emanating primarily from the activities of the human intellect. Any property, movable or immovable, is legally protected to prevent it from being stolen. Similarly, the rights in an intellectual property created need also to be protected to prevent infringement. Examples: Patents, design, trade marks and copy rights. The legal rights accrued on the intellectual property created are termed (intellectual property rights IPR). These rights are governed by the law on IPR of the country which grants such rights. There are various forms of IPR. The Trade Related Aspects of IPR popularly known as TRIPS, in the Agreement of the World Trade Organization (WTO), recognize seven forms of IPR, namely, patents, design, trade marks, copyrights, geographical indication, integrated circuits, and trade secrets.

Patents. These are legal rights granted for new inventions employing scientific and technical knowledge. Examples: A new drug for the treatment of AIDS and a new cell phone.

Industrial designs. A design is an idea or conception as to the features of shape, configuration pattern, ornament of composition of lines or colours applied to any article, two or three–dimensional or both by any industrial process or means which in the finished article appeals to and is judged solely by the eye or product. Example: Design as applied to shoes, TV, textiles.

Trade marks. A trade mark is a visual symbol in the form of a word, service or label applied to an article of a manufacturer or commerce with a view to indicating to the public the origin of manufacture of the goods affixed with that mark. It distinguishes such goods from others in the trade. *Examples*: Coca Cola in soft drinks, SONY in electronic goods.

Copyrights. A copyright is basically the right to copy and make use of literary, dramatic, musical, artistic works, cinematographic films, records and broadcasts. It is a proprietary right and comes into existence as soon as the work is created. The concept had its origin in the common law. Subsequently, it came to be governed by the statutory laws of each country. *Examples*: poems, artistic drawings, paintings, computer/programs.

Protection for new plant varieties. TRIPS provisions of the WTO Agreement make it mandatory for member countries to provide protection for new plant varieties. *Examples*: New variety of rice or wheat. The provisions have given member countries two options for providing protection to new plant varieties: (a) under the patent law itself, and (b) by a separate system (called Suigeneris system).

Geographical indications. Geographical indications identify goods as originating in the territory of a country, an origin or a locality in that territory, where a specific quality, reputations or other characteristics of the goods is essentially attributed to their geographical origin. *Example*: Darjeeling tea, Kancheepuram sari. The legal rights secured for an intellectual property under appropriate legislation can be enforced only within the boundaries of the country which grants such rights. For example, the rights secured by the grant of a patent in India can be enforced only in India. In other words, there is nothing like a world patent or an international patent. Hence, if one desires protection for an IP created for one's invention in different countries, one has to make separate applications in each country according to the law and practice prevailing in that country. In other words, the TRIPS provisions of the WTO Agreement do not envisage one patent that will be valid in all member countries. It is not necessary that a product/process (invention) should be protected under an appropriate IP law for its commercialization. The inventor has the right to commercialize the invention if the said invention is not already protected by somebody else. However, protection under IPR is considered essential for the promotion of technological, industrial and economical developments of a country as it provides incentives for the inventions and ensures adequate returns on commercialization of the invention. Among IP systems, patents can be said to be the most common, important and complicated ones because of their techno-legal nature and the widest and strongest legal protection one can secure. The benefits of the IP systems are, therefore, explained with reference to the patent system.

Patents are in addition to securing exclusive legal rights for the invention disclosed, and are useful for

1. advancing knowledge and bringing new knowledge eventually into the public domain through the unique source of information contained therein;
2. identifying the trends;
3. evaluating the strength of competitors;
4. identifying unexplored areas for undertaking R & D so as to become a leader in that area; and
5. identifying unprotected areas to avoid infringement.

IPR is now an integral part of economic life all over the world. All those who undertake scientific and technological research, those who create and interpret works of learning, culture, entertainment and information, those who devise marketing strategies for the products and services—all look to protection against piracy, to sustain what is distinctly theirs. The formidable task is to provide proprietary protection within global communication structures presaged by Internet. The major producing countries insist that IPR should become one ground rule of liberalization within the GATT. Hence, the TRIPs was included at the end of the Agreement of Uruguay Round in April 1994.

Indian scenario. In India there are four enactments:

1. The Patents Act 1970
2. The Copyrights Act 1957
3. Trade and Merchandise Marts Act 1958
4. The Design Act 1911

These are supported by a host of other supplementary acts and amendments. The new industrial policy of 1991 opened up India to economic acceleration. In this atmosphere, the transnational corporations which have stepped into India for trade in inventions, technologies, and services were concerned about legal protection; and so was the indigenous industry. In the Indian context, the Contract Act 1872, the laws of Torts are also relevant to the subject. The legislation concerned with the transfer of technology covers a number of other statutes and regulations like the Indian Companies Act 1956, Income Tax Act 1961, the MRTP Act 1969, the FERA (FTMA) as amended, and so on. Starting with Patent Law, the patent systems from the storehouse of technology. It provides the means of linking technological innovations to commerce. A patent for a particular invention is the grant of monopoly for the commercial or industrial exploitation of the invention by a person to whom it is granted. The patentee is entitled to license or sell his invention to others in return for loyalty. Patent is closely related to product or process technology, which is broadly classified to include (a) intangible property that can be legally protected; (b) technical know-how of product or process that cannot be patented because it is information not generally known.

The Indian Patent Act 1970, as amended by 1999 Act, deals with granting rights. The object of patent law is to encourage research and grant exclusive privileges to patentees. The patent law requires the patentee to disclose his invention fully and define clearly the exact invention. The details required to disclose are bibliographic information, description of invention, summary, brief description of the training needs and claims since the Indian Patent Act 1970 provides various checks to prevent invalid patents being granted right. Detailed scrutiny is done at the patent office and objection invited from the public. As soon as the application for the patent is advertised as accepted, the patent office makes the complete specification filed in pursuance of the application, open for public inspection and prints the same for public distribution. The Act provides publication of notification in the official gazette. These relate to various procedures like filing of application, acceptance of complete specification, opposition proceedings, sealing of patents, renewal fee payment, amendment proceedings, compulsory license proceedings, non-working patents, change in the name of applicant, declaration of intention by the Central Government regarding the revocation of a patent, etc. Novelty and utility are deemed as basic requisites of a patent. The Controller General of Patents, Designs and Trade Marks works on the patent information system.

The salient features of the Patents Act 1970 are:

- It codifies inventions which are not patenable.
- Patents can be granted for methods of process but not substance as per section, in respect of inventions relating to food, drugs and medicines, or substance prepared by chemical process.
- The period of validity of the patent of process relating to food, medicine and drugs is five years from the date of ceiling of patent or seven years from the date of patent, whichever is shorter. In case of others it is 14 years.
- It provides for endorsement of patent with the words "license of right".
- It provides for compulsory licensing on some other circumstances as well.
- It provides for use of invention for purpose of government and acquisition of invention by the Central Government.
- It provides for revocation of patents in public interest.

The UNCTAD has described the Indian Patents Act 1970 as the most progressive of the patent laws in the world. The Act consciously strives to strike a balance between the interests of the inventor and the consumer. It has now been amended by the 1999 Act, keeping in view the Indian government obligation under the Uruguay Round. Until 1994, there was no International organization to deal with trade issues between countries. Since the Bretten Woods Conference (1994) and drawing up of the GATT (1947), the International Trading System had functioned under GATT (General Agreement on Tariffs and Trade). The GATT conventions governed the multilateral trade. But GATT never had the standing of an International organization. It served only the signatories. The sudden change in Uruguay Round (1986–92) of trade negotiations under the GATT ended with an agreement to found the WTO. The WTO came into being on January 1, 1995 and has the same standing as the IMF and IBRD. The GATT articles were incorporated into WTO. It was a product of long GATT rounds of five decades. As a founder member of GATT since 1947, India has participated in seven negotiation rounds before the Uruguay Round but the Uruguay Round generated much heat in India and the name Arthur Dunkel, the author of Dunkel Draft, was tossed around by the Business press in 1993–94. The GATT presented threats and opportunities. It did not commit to free trade with zero tariffs, but was commited to removing barriers to world trade. Much of what the GATT accord required has in fact already been implemented in India as part of liberalization.

Chapter 7

Ethical Audit

In dealing with the responsibilities and meeting the ethical concerns at each stage in a project, the professional should be able to handle the conflicts that may arise within and between the stages, and between the interests of the several parties involved. Careful proactive planning will ensure that the consideration of potential conflicts is part of the development process, taking place, as far as possible, before the conflicts arise. It is important for the engineer to be aware of the values held by all the different parties in any situation and negotiate a general understanding of their several responsibilities and interests. Ethics, considered as the science of human relationships, is an examination of the quality of life of societies and of the impact of proposed actions upon this quality. Due consideration enables sound, just exchanges to take place. Unethical behaviour leads to conflicts, to the misuse of material and human resources to poor and careless workmanship and management, and to a lower quality of life for all affected.

Ethical behaviour based on the developed intrinsic virtues (integrity, independence, impartiality, responsibility, competence and discretion), and guided by the extrinsic directions of professional organizations, leads to the exercise of competence, efficiency and collaboration. These result in good workmanship and management, and to a higher quality of life for both those concerned with the execution of a project and those affected by it. To enable a systematic approach to be adopted for the resolution of questions which are essentially unquantifiable, it is useful to consider the normal stages of project realization and to review them against the professional rules of practice. Effectively, this involves carrying out an ethical audit of the project so that essential decisions can be made which include, in addition to the normal technical, economic and legal components, the ethical dimensions.

7.1 ASPECTS OF PROJECT REALIZATION

There are five aspects of project realization. They are:

1. The interests and roles of the decision makers
2. The brief
3. The context of realization—political, social, economic, and physical
4. The design
5. The implementation.

Each of these aspects presents a set of decisions which have ethical implications. We will identify the areas where conflicts may arise, and where consensus decisions may have to be negotiated. The best way to resolve conflicts is to avoid them in the first place. Good behaviour helps. Conflicts are symptoms of differences—i.e. of difference in understanding about intentions, of differing value systems, of differing cultures, from confusions between the aims of an action and the objects of the actors. All actions in which conflicts are generated arise from our relationships within communities of people, societies, and collaborative ventures. The structure and traditions of particular societies affect our moral judgements. The resolution of conflicts results in agreement. Agreement requires an acceptance of a common aim, rather than differing objectives. At each stage in the hierarchy of decisions, an increasingly large number of people in an ever-widening context are affected. It is important to appreciate the ranges of influence of decisions and, therefore, the range of understanding and objectivity required if decisions are to be 'good'. This appreciation should be present at the earliest possible stage in the development of a project. A 'good' decision is one that improves the quality of the output and of the lives of those concerned with its execution and its result.

It general, the areas of concern in civil engineering projects are those of society, humanity and the environment. Irresponsible performance can have adverse effects on the quality of life of many people not directly concerned with the project, and on the environment, certainly for many decades, if not for centuries to come. Conflicts at this level may become evident during public consultation or at formal planning inquiries, and should certainly form part of any audit.

7.2 ETHICAL AUDIT PROCEDURE

There are clear differences between the contractual obligations entered into by the several parties to a project, and the ethical duties of those parties. The project brief should set out the aims and constraints of the project, and the duties and obligations of the several parties, acknowledging the rewards and methods of payment for the services provided, and the quality of services and products expected. The temporary relationships, formal and informal, between the contracting parties during the lifetime of a particular project require careful consideration. The inclusion of an ethical section in every project brief will help reduce the conflicts that inevitably arise under the pressure of project execution. Such ethical reviews should be made a formal part of project procedures with time set aside to consider relationships, or any changes needed as the work proceeds. It is best that this review be independent of normal project team meetings, and not just included as a late item on an already crowded agenda. The time allocated for such reviews will be found to pay for itself many times over. It is certainly not just a public relations item. With a clear statement of values, each of the parties can carry out his individual duties with responsibility.

7.3 THE DECISION MAKERS

The avoidance of disputes and conflicts requires careful and willing collaboration between the parties involved, at the outset of any collaborative effort. There must be a clear understanding of the aim of the project—what need is being met, and what are the surrounding circumstances. Physical, financial and temporal restraints need to be clearly defined, and the nature of the contribution required from each member of the team, established and recorded as understood. It should be acknowledged that the individual parties may have differing objectives, and these should be clearly and openly defined. Clients of the construction industry are widely varied in size, function and organizational type. They may be individuals, corporate or public bodies. Each will have a distinct philosophy governing its objectives and the way it operates. Their priorities are likely to be radically different from those of their professional advisors. Clients may be experienced in the construction process or they may be inexperienced, having no previous knowledge of construction. A further distinction may also be made between clients whose main business involves construction projects—developers, industrial/manufacturing organizations, public sector agencies—and those whose involvement with construction is only an occasional event (extensions to their business properties). The client will require a construction which is fit for purpose, and one that is delivered in time and within an agreed budget. The consultant may wish to have a project which demonstrates his skill and can be provided within his fees. The contractor will prefer a project in which

- early agreement is required on broad parameters for the commercial viability of the project;
- flexible approaches are required to incorporating client changes during the design stage;
- 'open-book' approach to negotiations for prices of construction work is required, particularly for estimates of the cost of variations;
- agreement on detailed specifications is required for projects before the start of construction works;
- consideration must be given to the matter of standardization, to ease buildability;
- the use of independent professional project management, using experienced professionals, should be considered;

- structured total quality management (TQM)/Quality Assurance(QA) should be utilized; and
- good working relationships between parties and good communications are paramount.

7.4 VARIETY OF INTERESTS

The traditionally accepted construction philosophy has inevitably led to a redefinition of the duties, roles and responsibilities of the engineer. The roles may be less clearly defined and may generate some internal conflicts. However, conflicts arise under the traditional and the clearly defined roles of independent organizations of specialists—clients, consultants, suppliers, contractors, financiers, et al. In considering these diverse interests, it is helpful to take into account those factors that assist the reaching of common aims and standards—the integrating factors, and those conflicting factors that arise from differences. At the outset of any project, the client begins to assemble, probably with the assistance of his prime consultant, the team of advisors, suppliers and contractors with the necessary skills to achieve his objectives. The following factors relate to the development of such a team:

- It is unlikely that any one advisor will have the skills and knowledge necessary to develop a project. Briefing becomes a team effort as professionals with specific expertise or experience are introduced to the project. Many of these will form part of a permanent project team; others may be retained only as long as their inputs are required.
- The project and design teams may comprise many specialist disciplines, civil, structural, mechanical and electrical engineers, architects, land surveyors, economists, et al. depending on the scope and magnitude of the project.
- The number of parties involved in a project may well reach a level at which a project coordinator or project manager will be formally appointed. This is frequently the case.
- As the aims and means of achieving them in a project are established and developed, the scheme is subject to appraisal in terms of its viability. Sketch designs will be prepared by the design team and a strategic programme prepared, reflecting the clients' aims, completion date, financial targets, and quality standards.
- Each member of the team, including the client, will be faced with a variety of problems and each will offer solutions based on their background, experience and professional training. The project manager will focus the analyses of these problems in the context of the overall project goals, presenting the alternatives to the client for approval.
- These discussions will involve or be influenced by the views and concerns of external organizations and interested parties, many of whom

may be affected by the project during its planning, construction or operational stages, and in the long or short-term. Their concerns may include social considerations such as employment, health and safety, education, cultural or recreational activities, security, displacement and relocation. They may also be interested in the environmental or other aspects of the project.

In all these situations, the engineer who may be playing any one of several roles—client, or consultant, public agent, or contractor—must assess his own duties and responsibilities relative to those roles. The ethical audit will identify the roles of the various parties and attempt to define their responsibilities within the total procurement process.

7.5 FORMULATION OF THE BRIEF

Projects of all sizes involve the appraisal and consideration of a multitude of constraints—technical, legal, financial, environmental, organizational and ethical. The client's brief will ultimately define the priorities and objectives of the project. Without a comprehensive brief, no project can be successful. The brief is usually prepared in an interactive dialogue between the client and his advisor, with the advisor obtaining and clarifying information from the client. Part of this information may be obvious and easy to access. Much may be unclear and the client may not appreciate its relevance or the advisor in the context of the project. The preparation of the brief requires careful consideration not only to meet the needs appropriately but to avoid ethical conflicts arising from partial views or misunderstandings.

At the inception stage of any project the client perceives a need. This will be a response to the situation in which his organization operates. Generally, the need will be to combine many forces and stimuli including the need to survive, to maintain position in relation to competitors, and economic or sociological forces. These needs trigger the start of a construction project—although construction professionals may not be involved initially. At this time the client probably has little information on what he requires from the project, other than a broad estimate of how much money is available for the works and an approximate idea of the time at which he requires the project to be completed and operating.

For many clients approaching a construction project, there will be feelings of vulnerability based on

- working outside their own field of expertise or knowledge;
- placing themselves in the hands of professionals who may not be using working methods and technologies that the client may not understand or have trouble in controlling;
- uncertainty as to the feasibility or programme of the project; and
- knowledge that they may be embarking on a complex process with high risks.

The client will require 'value for money' measured in terms of time, quality and price. The relative importance of these three parameters will vary from client to client, and each will be willing to make 'tradeoffs' between the three in order to achieve his own particular organization's goals. The client will require the assistance of professional advisors to help him appraise the feasibility and viability of his plans and ultimately to assist him to construct the project, should he decide to go ahead. He will aim to pass some of the risks involved in the project onto his advisors and the constructor. He will expect the advisors to provide sound independent advice and information in a form that he can understand and which can be used to help him to make decisions. He also expects his advisors to understand his needs, context, and operational aims and structure so that their advice will be relevant. The focus of these needs may be internal to his organization and may conflict with the broader outward looking views of his advisors.

7.5.1 The Environment

Individuals living together in societies improve the quality of their lives by their corporate efforts and their shared skills and talents. Such efforts frequently lead to misery and distress is evident; but this may be more often the result of ignorance and greed than a reflection of the nature of societies in general. Engineering projects inevitably impact not only on the physical, but also on the economic and social 'environments' that contain them. 'Environments' include all the factors outside the project that may affect or be affected by the project. These impacts may be beneficial or they may be harmful. Modern engineers must now also take into account finite resources and the complex interaction of the project and its environment—social and physical.

Engineers are therefore responsible not only for the effective use, management and conservation of the resources placed at their disposal within the project, but also for the analysis of the project within a complex and changing external environment. Well drafted contract documents contribute greatly to clarity and the anticipation of possible areas of difficulty, enabling possible conflicts to be resolved before they arise. The types of issue that can cause conflict, for example, include a need to change a material supplier, the need for extended working hours, the introduction of unplanned construction techniques—blasting, open cut substitution for tunnelling, etc. Site hygiene and safety are the responsibility of the site management, and are part of the overall professional responsibility for all engineers involved in the project. Labour relationships require consideration and fairness. Adequate provision needs to be made for the training of all operatives and the management staff, in that regard. It can be helpful to hold initial, and perhaps regular meetings at which the designers or owners can explain to the site operatives why certain decisions have been made, the sequence of operations, the importance of quality control and perhaps to encourage feedback from 'grass-roots' on suggestions for improvements in working procedures.

7.6 THE AUDIT STATEMENT

It is of value to set down the details of the project, not only at the outset of the development, but as they are revealed or changed during the lifetime of the work. The continuous appraisal of the current state of the work is most important. The past is only of relevance if it informs us of present situations or suggests possible outcomes for alternative lines of developments. The clearly established aims of the project will suggest lines of action proceeding from the known situation to the desired ends. A special meeting considering only ethical aspects of the project can be of great help. Failing this, adequate time must be set aside for their consideration during other meetings. Continuous attention to the details can reduce the time required to resolve problems to a minimum, ensuring smoother running of the contracts. Special aspects of particular projects, and standard agenda can be developed for such review meetings, with particular individuals identified to report on differing sections of the work.

7.7 THE AUDIT REVIEWS

There are two types of review meeting—the construction team meeting, and the consultative meeting with local interested parties.

The report format for the ethical audit should be in two parts, namely,

- a review of the present situation
- the ethical implications of future activities.

The object of the audit or ethical brief is to identify possible points of future conflicts of interest and to eliminate them wherever possible. The records and recommendations can be divided usefully into five stages:

1. *Schedules of all parties concerned* — to include names, addresses, etc., and management structures of each organization with deputies named for each key player. The roles, responsibilities and reporting paths of all the main 'actors' should be defined — clients, managers, consultants, contractors, suppliers, design/build/supply orgainzations, statutory officers, etc. This should include details of subcontractors with records of their contractual relationships with main contractors.
2. *The agreed briefs* — summaries of briefs for all sections of the project, including programme limitations, should be included in the ethical files. Special note must be made of any performance specifications and of any special constraints (e.g. on suppliers, country of origin, materials, safety standards, security, and confidentiality). Quality management procedures need to be set out with definitions of the responsibilities and authorities of those concerned with the monitoring of quality.

3. *The context*—in addition to a full description of the site and of those aspects of the neighbouring communities likely to be affected by the work, records should include full details of any environmental impact assessment that has been carried out, with the recommendations carefully noted. Are there any special requirements concerning working conditions, health and safety, security, pollution, communications, traffic management, restrictions on working hours, etc.?

Statutory and legal requirements should be noted with definitions of any national or international standards to be observed. In some cases when operating between, or in, different nation-states, a special section identifying any unusual aspects of the law should be noted. Relationships with approving bodies (planners, by-laws, etc.) need to be defined, and where no local regulations exist, agreement needs to be reached and recorded on standards of working practices to be observed.

4. *The design* — any special requirements for reversibility, sustainability, energy conservation, etc., need to be noted. Variations in design during construction are not unknown, and the original criteria need to be available for reference, e.g. capital vs. maintenance criteria and whole-life costing. The contract documents and detailed specifications and instructions issued should clearly define and instruct contractors and suppliers on their contractual obligations. Careful attention should be given to the interface between the parts of the project, particularly if work on these is to be undertaken by different parties, perhaps separated by some interval of time.
5. *Implementation* — the items covering relationships with local communities and the construction aspects of the project should be noted and reviewed as a matter of routine at the regular meetings on ethical, or working practices. Trade union relationships should be noted, with reports on security and safety. Problems with the delivery and supply of materials and components, or of dust and noise light pollution, should be resolved.

The identification and definition of possible sources of differences can reduce conflicts to a minimum and ensure that trust between all parties, with respect for their particular interests and contributions, underpins all the work, and results in a sound project, delivered to programme and budget, to the satisfaction of all concerned.

Review Questions

UNIT I: Engineering Ethics/Introduction

Short Questions

1. Discuss the need to focus on Professional Ethics.
2. Define Personal and Professional Ethics.
3. What is meant by *moral autonomy*?
4. Classify the types of inquiry.
5. Define the terms 'profession' and 'professionalism'.
6. What are the basic concepts of right action?
7. What do you understand by self-interest and ethical egoism?
8. Explain the levels of moral development suggested by Kohlberg?
9. What are the steps needed in confronting moral dilemmas?
10. Which are the practical skills that will help to produce effective independent thought about moral issues?
11. What are the three virtues of religion?
12. What are the professional responsibilities?
13. What is the ethical duty of a manager toward his fellow engineer?
14. Explain what is meant by moral integrity.
15. What is self-respect?
16. Explain the concepts of Rule Utilitarianism and Rational Desires.
17. Explain Kant's view of duty ethics.
18. What are the membership criteria for being an engineer?

Long Questions

1. Discuss any two case studies on professional disagreements an engineer may encounter and discuss how you would act in that situation.
2. Discuss the scope and aims of engineering ethics.

3. Discuss the theories pertaining to Moral Autonomy with specific reference to consensus and controversy.
4. What is meant by professional responsibility and discuss the theories about virtues.
5. Where and how do moral problems arise in engineering?
6. What is virtue ethics? Explain the meaning of virtue and the "golden mean" of Aristotle.
7. What are the theories about morality? Explain briefly about each theory.

UNIT II: Moral Reasoning and Ethical Theories

Short Questions

1. What are the theories of right action?
2. Differentiate between act and rule utilitarianism.
3. Distinguish between duty ethics and right ethics.
4. What are the uses of ethical theories?
5. Distinguish between normative, conceptual and factual inquiries.
6. How management decision is different from engineering decision?
7. What is meant by sustainability?
8. Define moral dilemma and moral residue.
9. What is universalizability?

Long Questions

1. Explain Kohlberg's model of moral development.
2. Explain Gilligan theory of moral development.
3. Explain Moral disagreement, moral absolutism moral relativism and moral pluralism.
4. Compare and contrast act-oriented and character-oriented ethics.
5. Explain compassion and caring.

UNIT III: Engineering as Social Experimentation

Short Questions

1. Explain the meaning of Accountability.
2. What are the functions of code of ethics?
3. What are the limitations of code of ethics?
4. What is the role played by experimentation in the design process?
5. Give a brief account of learning from the past, mentioning at least two examples.
6. What do you understand by experimental control?
7. What is said to be a 'regulated society'?
8. Write short notes on Industrial Standards.
9. What do you understand by the term 'authenticity'?
10. Define 'control group'.
11. What are the responsibilities of engineers to society?

12. Define 'conscientiousness'.
13. What is the role of an engineer in responsible experimentation?
14. Discuss Moral Autonomy and accountability.
15. Discuss the prerequisites that an engineer should have to be a responsible experimenter.

Long Questions

1. Compare and contrast engineering experiments with standard experiments.
2. Discuss the problems of law vis-a-vis engineering.
3. What is the proper role of law in engineering?
4. What are the aspects of engineering that make it appropriate to view engineering projects as experiments?
5. Explain, with the help of examples that engineers would learn not only from their earlier design and operating results, but also from those of other engineers.
6. What are the general features of morally responsible engineers ? Explain each feature with appropriate examples.
7. In the Challenger Disaster, examine if and how the principal actors behaved as responsible experimenters.
8. What are said to be the main elements included in 'informed consent'? Enumerate the conditions that would define valid consent.
9. Summarize the relationship between the codes and the experimental nature of engineering in concurrence with the limitations.

UNIT IV: Engineer's Responsibility for Safety

Short Questions

1. Distinguish the attitude of different types of consumers with regard to safety and comment on it.
2. Write short notes on the concept of safety.
3. How far and up to what level can we accept risk in a product?
4. Discuss some of the possible ways we can reduce risk.
5. What degree of risk is acceptable?
6. What would be the uncertainities encountered in a design process?
7. How are involuntary personal risks assessed?
8. What are the faulty assumptions about safety?
9. "Safety in a product comes with a price". Explain.
10. What do you understand by 'acceptable' risks?
11. What is meant by 'voluntary risks'?
12. Mention the incentives to reduce risks?
13. What is meant by 'acceptability of risk'?
14. Write short notes on liability.
15. Explain job related risks.
16. How can risks be reduced? Explain.

Long Questions

1. Explain in detail about the effect of information on risk assessments.
2. Discuss in detail the testing strategies for safety.
3. Describe in detail the concept of 'Risk-Benefit Analysis'.
4. Would knowledge of risk help you to have better safety standards or safe products? Substantiate your argument with suitable case studies.
5. How to account publicly for benefits and risks?
6. Discuss the notion of 'safe exit' using evacuation plans for communities near nuclear power plants or chemical processing plants.
7. What are the safety lessons we can learn from Three mile island and Chernobyl safe exits?

UNIT V: Responsibilities and Rights

Short Questions

1. "A person who is loyal has respect for authority". Discuss.
2. "Professional rights can lead to conflicts of interest". Explain.
3. What is meant by 'whistle blowing'?
4. List any two limitations of 'whistle blowing'.
5. List the moral rights of a salaried engineer.
6. What is meant by loyalty and collegiality?
7. Define the word 'confidentiality'.
8. Write short notes on occupational crime.
9. Define Utilitarianism.
10. Differentiate copyright and patent.
11. What is meant by 'discrimination'?
12. State the benefits of collective bargaining.
13. Discuss the relationship between professional responsibility and loyalty to company.
14. Define 'privileged information' and 'proprietary information'.
15. What is the right of professional conscience?
16. What is 'reverse discrimination'?

Long Questions

1. How are 'conflicts of interest' solved?
2. Discuss in detail about the 'employee rights'.
3. What is the importance of loyalty and collegiality in team work?
4. What are the procedures to be followed for 'whistle blowing'? How can this be avoided?
5. Discuss the ways and means of reducing occupational crime in industries.
6. What is institutional authority? How do you correlate institutional authority, expert authority, and power?
7. Explain the meaning of faithful agent in relation to public service.

8. Discuss the right of conscientious refusal.
9. Explain what is needed by the right to recognition.
10. Define and elucidate on Intellectual Property Rights.
11. What is respect for authority? How far should it be recognized by salaried professionals as morally justified?

UNIT VI: Global Issues

Short Questions

1. What is meant by 'Globalization'?
2. What is contextualism?
3. What are the three senses of relative values?
4. Enumerate the international rights as suggested by Donaldson.
5. What is 'technology transfer' and 'appropriate technology'?
6. How do you internalize the costs of environmental degradation?
7. Explain the meaning of 'moral leadership'.
8. What is meant by 'voluntarism'?

Long Questions

1. Does globalization solve the global issues?
2. Explain the role of engineers as managers.
3. Explain the meaning of environmental ethics.
4. What is meant by computer ethics?
5. Discuss the pros and cons of multinational companies (MNCs) from the ethical point of view.
6. Explain engineers as expert witnesses and advisors.
7. What are the philosophical views of nature? Discuss ecocentric ethics.
8. Discuss an engineers involvement in weapons work.
9. What is meant by 'morally creative leaders' and participation in professional societies?
10. Write a brief account on 'consulting engineering'.
11. Define patent, industrial design, trade mark and copy right.
12. Explain intellectual property rights (IPR).
13. What is the Indian Scenario?
14. Explain the salient features of Indian Patent Act, 1970.

UNIT VII: Ethical Audit

1. What is Ethical Audit?
2. What is Project realization and explain the five aspects of the same?
3. Explain the ethical audit procedure.
4. How will you formulate brief for a project?
5. Explain Audit Review.

CASE STUDIES

Case Study 1

Space Shuttle Challenger

On January 28, 1986, the Space Shuttle Challenger was launched for the last time. The decision to launch the Challenger was not simple. Certainly no one dreamed that the Shuttle would explode less than two minutes after lift-off. Much has been said and written about the decision to launch the Space Shuttle. Was the decision to launch correct? How was the decision made? Could anyone have foreseen the subsequent explosion? Should the decision-making procedure have been modified? These questions are examined in this case study.

Background

The Space Shuttle is the most complicated vehicle ever constructed. Its complexity dwarfs any previous project ever attempted, including the Apollo project. The Apollo project possessed a very specific goal—to send men to the moon—whereas the Space Shuttle program had a wide variety of goals, some of which were in conflict. The attempt to satisfy conflicting goals was one of the chief roots of difficulty with the design of the Space Shuttle. Originally, the design was to be only a part of NASA's overall manned space transportation system, but because of politics and budget cuts, it was transformed from an integral component of a system to the sole component of the manned space program.

The Space Shuttle was the first attempt to produce a truly reusable spacecraft. All previous spacecraft were designed to fly only a single mission. In the late 1960s, NASA envisioned a vehicle that could be used repeatedly, thus reducing both the engineering cost and hardware costs. However, the resulting vehicle was not as envisioned. It had severe design flaws, one of which caused the loss of the Challenger.

NASA—PLANNING AND POLITICS

NASA's post-Apollo plans for the continued manned exploration of space rested on a three-legged triad. The first leg was a reusable space-transportation system, the Space Shuttle, which could transport men and cargo to low earth orbit (LEO) and then land back on Earth to prepare for another mission. The second leg was a manned orbiting space station that would be re-supplied by the Shuttle and would serve as both a transfer point for activities further from Earth and as a scientific and manufacturing platform. The final leg was the exploration of Mars, which would start from the Space Station. Unfortunately, the politics and inflation of the early 70s forced NASA to retreat from its ambitious program. Both the Space Station and the Journey to Mars were delayed indefinitely, and the United States Manned Space Program was left standing on one leg—the Space Shuttle. Even worse, the Shuttle was constantly under attack by a Democratic Congress and poorly defended by a Republican president.

To retain Shuttle funding, NASA was forced to make a series of major concessions. First, facing a highly constrained budget, NASA sacrificed the research and development necessary to produce a truly reusable shuttle and instead accepted a design that was only partially reusable, eliminating one of the features that made the shuttle attractive in the first place. Solid Rocket Boosters (SRBs) were used instead of safer liquid fueled boosters because they required a much smaller research-and-development effort. Numerous other design changes were made to reduce the level of research and development required.

Second, to increase its political clout and to guarantee a steady customer base, NASA enlisted the support of the United States Air Force. The Air Force could provide the considerable political clout of the Defense Department and had many satellites which required launching. However, Air Force support did not come without a price. The Shuttle payload bay was required to meet Air Force size and shape requirements, which placed key constraints on the ultimate design. Even more important was the Air Force requirement that the Shuttle be able to launch from Vandenburg Air Force Base in California. This constraint required a larger cross range than the Florida site, which in turn decreased the total allowable vehicle weight. The weight reduction required the elimination of the design's air-breathing engines, resulting in a single-pass unpowered landing that greatly limited the safety and landing versatility of the vehicle.

FACTORS AFFECTING THE LAUNCH DECISION

1. Pressures to fly. As the year 1986 began, there was extreme pressure on NASA to "Fly out the Manifest" From its inception, the Space Shuttle program had been plagued by exaggerated expectations, funding inconsistencies, and political pressures. The ultimate design was shaped almost as much by politics as by physics. President Kennedy's declaration that the United States would land a man on the moon before the end of the decade had provided NASA's Apollo program with high visibility, a clear direction, and powerful political backing. The Space Shuttle program was not as fortunate; it had neither a clear direction nor consistent political backing.

2. System status and competition. In spite of all its early difficulties, the Shuttle program looked quite good in 1985. A total of 19 flights had been launched and recovered, and although many had experienced minor problems, all but one of the flights could rightfully be categorized as successful. However, delays in the program as a whole had led the Air Force to request funds to develop an expendable launch vehicle. Worse still, the French launch organization Arian Space had developed an independent capability to place satellites into orbit at prices the Shuttle could not hope to match without greatly increased federal subsidization (which was not likely to happen as the Congress was becoming increasingly dissatisfied with the program). The Shuttle was soon going to have to begin showing that it could pay for itself. There was only one way this could be done—increase the number of flights.

For the Shuttle program, 1986 was to be the year of truth. NASA had to prove that it could launch a large number of flights on time to continue to attract customers and retain Congressional support. Unfortunately, 1986 did not started out well for the Shuttle program. Columbia, Flight 61-C, had experienced a record four on-pad aborts and had three other schedule slips. Finally, on Mission 61-C, Columbia was forced to land at Edwards Air Force Base rather than at Kennedy Space Center as planned. The delays in Columbia's launch and touchdown threatened to upset the launch schedule for the rest of the year.

Not only did Columbia's landing at Edwards require it to be carried back to the Cape, but several key shuttle parts had to be carried back by T-38 for use on the other vehicles. These parts included a temperature sensor for the propulsion system, the nose-wheel steering box, an air sensor for the crew cabin, and one of the five general-purpose computers. At the time of the Challenger explosion, NASA supposedly had four complete shuttles. In reality there were only enough parts for two complete shuttles. Parts were passed around and reinstalled in the orbiters with the earliest launch dates. Each time a part was removed or inserted, the shuttles were exposed to a whole host of possible servicing-induced problems.

In addition to problems caused by the Flight 61-C of Columbia, the next Columbia flight, 61-E, scheduled for March, also put pressure on NASA to launch the Challenger on schedule. The March flight of Columbia was to carry the ASTRO spacecraft, which had a very tight launch window because NASA wanted it to reach Halley's Comet before a Russian probe arrived at the comet. In order to launch Columbia 61-E on time, Challenger had to carry out its mission and return to Kennedy Space Center by January 31.

3. Politics. NASA had much to gain from a successful Flight 51-L. The "Teacher in Space" mission had generated much more press interest than other recent shuttle flights. Publicity was and continues to be extremely important to the agency. It is a very important tool that NASA uses to help ensure its funding. The recent success of the Space Shuttle program had left NASA in a Catch-22 situation. Successful Shuttle flights were no longer news because they were almost ordinary. However, launch aborts and delayed landings were more newsworthy because they were much less common.

In addition to general publicity gained from flight 51-L, NASA undoubtedly was aware that a successful mission would play well in the White House. President Reagan shared NASA's love of publicity and was about to give a State of the Union speech. The value of an elementary teacher giving a lecture from orbit was obvious and was lost neither on NASA nor on President Reagan.

4. Sequence of events

MONDAY, JANUARY 27

On Monday January 27, NASA had attempted to place Challenger in orbit, only to be stymied by a stripped bolt and high winds. All preliminary procedures had been completed and the crew had just boarded when the first problem struck. A microsensor on the hatch indicated that it was not shut securely; it turned out that the hatch had been shut securely and that the sensor was malfunctioning, but valuable time was used determining that the sensor was the problem.

After the hatch was closed, the external hatch handle could not be removed. The threads on the connecting bolt were stripped, and instead of cleanly disengaging when turned, the handle simply spun around. Attempts to use a portable drill to remove the handle failed. Technicians on the scene asked Mission Control for permission to saw the bolt off. Fearing some form of structural stress to the hatch, engineers made numerous time-consuming calculations before giving the go-ahead to cut off the bolt. The entire process consumed almost two hours before the countdown was resumed.

Misfortunes continued. During the attempts to verify the integrity of the hatch and remove the handle, the wind had been steadily rising. Chief Astronaut John Young flew a series of approaches in the Shuttle training aircraft and confirmed the worst fears of Mission Control. The crosswinds at the Cape were in excess of the level allowed for the abort contingency. The opportunity had been missed and the flight would have to wait until the next possible launch window, the following morning. Everyone was quite discouraged, especially since extremely cold weather was forecast for Tuesday, which could further postpone the launch.

TUESDAY, JANUARY 28

After the cancelled launch on Monday morning, there was a great deal of concern about the possible effects of weather. The predicted low for Tuesday morning was 23°F, far below the nominal operating temperature for many of the Challenger's subsystems. Undoubtedly, as the sun came up and the launch time approached, both air temperature and vehicle would warm up, but there was still concern. Would the ambient temperature become high enough to meet launch requirements? NASA's Launch Commit Criteria stated that no launch should occur at temperatures below 31°F. There was also concern over any permanent effects on the Shuttle due to the cold overnight temperatures.

All NASA centers and subcontractors involved with the Shuttle were asked to determine the possible effects of cold weather and present any concerns. In the meantime, the Kennedy Space Center went ahead with its freeze-protection plan. This plan included using anti-freeze in the huge acoustic damping ponds and allowing warm water to bleed through pipes, showers, and hoses to prevent freezing.

The weather for Tuesday morning was to be clear and cold. Because the overnight low was forecast at 23°F, there was doubt that Challenger would be much above freezing at launch time. The Launch Commit Criteria included very specific temperature limits for most systems on the shuttle. A special waiver would be required to launch if any of these criteria were not met. Although these criteria were supposedly legally binding, the Marshall Space Flight Center administrator, Larry Mulloy had been routinely writing waivers to cover the problems with the SRBs on the recent Shuttle flights.

Engineers at Morton-Thiokol, the SRB manufacturer in Utah, were very concerned about the possible effects of the cold weather. The problems with the SRBs had been long known to engineers Roger Boisjoly and Allan McDonald, but both felt that their concerns were being ignored. They felt that the request by NASA to provide comment on the launch conditions was a golden opportunity to present their concerns. They were sure that the Challenger should not be launched in such conditions as those expected for Tuesday morning. Using weather data provided by the Air Force, they calculated that at the 9:00 a.m. launch time the temperature of the O-rings would be only 29°F. Even by 2:00 p.m., the O-rings would have warmed only to 38°F.

The design validation tests originally done by Thiokol covered only a very narrow temperature range. The temperature data base did not include any temperatures below 53°F. The O-rings from Flight 51-C, which had been launched under cold conditions the previous year, showed very significant erosion. This was the only data available on the effects of cold, but all the Thiokol engineers agreed that the cold weather would decrease the elasticity of the synthetic rubber O-rings, which in turn might cause them to seal slowly and allow hot combustion gas to surge through the joint.

Based on these results, the engineers at Thiokol recommended to NASA Marshall that Challenger not be launched until the O-rings reached a temperature of 53°F. The management of Marshall was flabbergasted, and demanded that

Thiokol prove that launching was unsafe. Such a response was a complete reversal of normal procedure. Normally, NASA required its subcontractors to prove that something was safe. Now they were requiring their subcontractors to prove that something was unsafe. Faced with this extreme pressure, Thiokol management asked its engineers to reconsider their position. When the engineers stuck to their original recommendations not to fly, Thiokol management overruled them and gave NASA its approval to launch.

Rockwell, the company that manufactured the Orbiter, also had concerns about launching in cold and icy conditions. Their major concern was the possibility of ice from either the Shuttle or the launch structure striking and damaging the vehicle. Like Thiokol, they recommended against the launch, and they too were pressed to explain their reasoning. Instead of sticking with their original strong recommendation against launch, the Rockwell team carefully worded their statement to say that they could not fully guarantee the safety of the Shuttle.

In its desire to fly out its manifest, NASA was willing to accept Rockwell's statement as a recommendation. The final decision to launch, however, belonged to Jesse Moore. He was informed of Rockwell's concerns, but was also told that they had approved the launch. The engineers and management from NASA Marshall chose not to even mention the original concerns of Thiokol. Somehow, the warnings and concerns were diminished as they were communicated at each step of the ladder of responsibility.

Late Monday night the decision to push onward with the launch was made. Despite the very real concerns of some of the engineers familiar with the actual vehicle subsystems, the launch was approved. No one at NASA wanted to be responsible for further delaying an already delayed launch. Everyone was aware of the pressure on the agency to fly out the manifest, yet no one would have consciously risked the lives of the seven astronauts. The potential rewards had come to outweigh the potential risks. Clearly, there were many reasons for launching Challenger on that cold Tuesday morning, and a great deal of frustration from the previous launch attempt remained.

Pre-Launch Events

Although the decision to launch on Tuesday had been made late on Monday night, it was still possible that something might force NASA to postpone the launch. However, the decision to launch had been made, and nothing was going to stand in the way; the "press on" mentality was firmly established, and even if all of Florida froze over, Challenger would be launched.

The pre-launch inspection of Challenger and the launch pad by the ice-team was unusual to say the least. The ice-team's responsibility was to remove any frost or ice on the vehicle or launch structure. What they found during their inspection looked like something out of a science-fiction movie. The freeze protection plan implemented by the Kennedy personnel had gone very wrong. Hundreds of icicles, some up to 16 in. long, clung to the launch structure. The handrails and walkways near the shuttle entrance were covered in ice, making them extremely dangerous if the crew had to make an emergency evacuation. One solid sheet of ice stretched from the 195 ft level to the 235 ft level on the gantry. However, NASA continued to cling to its calculations that there would be no damage due to flying ice shaken loose during the launch.

The Launch

As the SRBs ignited, the cold conditions did not allow the O-rings to properly seat. Within the first 300 milliseconds of ignition, both the primary and secondary O-rings on the lowest section of the right SRB were vaporized across 70° of arc by the hot combustion gases. Puffs of smoke with the same frequency as the vibrating booster are clearly present in pictures of the launch. However, soon after the Challenger cleared the tower, a temporary seal of glassy aluminum-oxides from the propellant formed in place of the burned O-rings and Challenger continued skyward.

Unfortunately, at the time of greatest dynamic pressure, the shuttle encountered wind shear. As the Challenger's guidance control lurched the Shuttle to compensate for the wind shear, the fragile aluminum-oxide seal shattered. Flame arched out of the joint, struck the external tank and quickly burned through the insulation and the aluminum structure. Liquid Hydrogen fuel streamed out and was ignited. The Challenger exploded.

When the remains of the cabin were recovered, it became apparent that most of the crew survived the explosion and separation of the Shuttle from the rest of the vehicle. During the 2 min. 45 sec. fall to the ocean, at least four of the personal egress packs were activated and at least three were functioning when the Challenger struck the water. The high-speed impact with the water produced a force of 200 g, and was undoubtedly the cause of death for all the crew.

Post-Crash Events

Since the crash of Challenger, NASA and external investigators have taken a look at both the shuttle and the sequence of events that allowed it to be launched. The SRBs have gone through significant redesign and now include a capture feature on the field joint. The three Marshall administrators most responsible for allowing the SRB problems to go uncorrected have all left NASA. Following the recommendations of the Rogers commission, NASA has attempted to streamline and clean up its communication lines. A system for reporting suspected problems anonymously now exists within NASA. In addition, the astronauts themselves are now much more active in many decision-making aspects of the program. The current NASA Administrator, Admiral Richard Truly, is a former shuttle astronaut.

Safety and Ethics Issues

There are many questions involving safety and/or ethics that are raised when we examine the decision to launch the Challenger. Obviously, the situation was unsafe. The ethics questions are more complex. If high standards of ethical conduct are to be maintained, then each person must differentiate between right and wrong and must follow the course that is determined to be the right, or ethical, course. Frequently, the determination of right or wrong is not simple, and good arguments can be made on both sides of the question. Some of the issues raised by the Challenger launch decision are as follows:

1. Are solid rocket boosters inherently too dangerous to use on manned spacecraft? If so, why are they a part of the design?
2. Was safety traded for political acceptability in the design of the Space Shuttle?
3. Did the pressure to succeed cause too many things to be promised to too many people during the design of the Space Shuttle?
4. Did the need to maintain the launch schedule force decision makers to compromise safety in the launch decision?
5. Were responsibilities being ignored in the writing of routine launch waivers for the Space Shuttle?
6. Were managers at Rockwell and Morton Thiokol wise (or justified) in ignoring the recommendations of their engineers?
7. Did the engineers at Rockwell and Morton Thiokol do all that they could to convince their own management and NASA of the dangers of launch?
8. When NASA pressed its contractors to launch, did it violate its responsibility to ensure crew safety?

When NASA discounted the effects of the weather, did it violate its responsibility to ensure crew safety?

Challenger Launch Decision Assignments

The problem faced by NASA managers on January 28, 1986, is simply stated: given the existing weather conditions, the recommendations of the various engineering and operational groups, and the political pressures, should Challenger be launched? Many conflicting factors were considered in reaching the decision to launch. Those responsible for high-risk programs such as Challenger must attempt to identify and evaluate the risks. Specific questions which needed to be answered were: 1. What level of risk was acceptable for launch? 2. Did the current conditions meet this standard? Even properly identifying and evaluating all risks is not sufficient because the potential benefits of taking each risk must be considered. Greater risks can sometimes be justified given the possibility of greater rewards. In the case of the Challenger, the people with the ultimate authority to launch came to the conclusion that the potential rewards justified what they believed to be relatively minor risks. The belief that the risks were minor, however, was not shared by many of the engineers further down the chain of responsibility.

Assignment A. Read the General Information provided on the Space Shuttle Challenger launch decision. Consider each of the following questions carefully in light of that information and write a paragraph, each answering each questions.

1. Why did NASA decide to launch Challenger?
2. How safe is safe enough? How does one determine what is an acceptable risk?
3. Is it possible to develop a methodology for quantifying risks, or must each particular situation be addressed individually?
4. Were NASA administrators justified in writing Launch Commit Criteria Waivers for Challenger and previous shuttle flights?
5. At the time of the Challenger accident there was a general feeling among both NASA and the public that the space shuttle was no longer an experimental vehicle, but was by then a fully operational vehicle, in the same sense as a commercial airliner. Was this a correct perception and why was it common?
6. Should someone have stopped the Challenger launch? If so, how could an individual have accomplished this?
7. If you were on a jury attempting to place liability, who would you say was responsible for the deaths of the astronauts? Are several individuals or groups liable?
8. How could the Morton-Thiokol engineers have convinced NASA and their own management to postpone the launch?
9. How can an engineer deal with pressure from above to follow a course of action he knows to be wrong?
10. How could the chains of communication and responsibility for the shuttle program have been made to function better?

Assignment B. Choose one of the following statements, research the topic, and write a two-page answer in which you explore the impact of the topic on the Challenger explosion.

1. Following Apollo, the manned space program suffered from lack of funding and direction.
2. The design for the space shuttle is a series of compromises driven by poorly timed allocations of funds from Congress.
3. To minimize R & D costs, only part of the shuttle system was made reusable, and solid boosters were used instead of the safer liquid boosters.
4. NASA was under intense pressure at the time of the Challenger accident to prove that the shuttle was a viable launch vehicle.
5. A significant delay in launching Challenger would have upset the launch schedule for the rest of the year.

6. Flight 51-L (Challenger) was scrubbed the previous day, leaving all involved frustrated and determined to launch it as soon as possible.
7. No test data on any of the shuttle components existed for the low overnight or launch temperatures.
8. Problems with the seals on the SRBs had been known for several flights and waivers had been written for each flight.
9. Concerns about the O-rings were never revealed to the NASA administrators who had the final launch authority.
10. Morton-Thiokol initially recommended against launch, but when pressured by NASA, reversed its decision.
11. The anti-freeze plan left large sheets of ice and icicles all over the launch structure. An analysis done at Houston showed no danger at lift-off due to falling ice.
12. Rockwell could not guarantee the shuttle's safety, but did not veto the launch. Their ice analysis showed some possibility of danger.
13. The ice team recommended against launching, but was overruled by Mission Control.

Assignment C. Divide the class into small groups, no more than three to a group. Each group is to choose one of the four roles outlined below and develop a statements outlining the position represented by those in your role on January 28, 1986. Develop two statements: 1. what you think was the position of those in your role. 2. The position that those in your role should have taken.

1. *NASA management:* You want to launch the Challenger as soon as possible. The delays are not only embarrassing, but threaten your funding and customer base. Challenger must launch on Tuesday to preserve the schedule. An analysis done by your engineers at Houston shows that the ice on the pad should not strike the Challenger when it lifts off.

2. *Thiokol engineers:* You believe it is not safe to launch, but have no hard data to back this up. Limited data from a previous cold weather flight indicates that temperature is important. Basic physics tells you that the O-rings will lose elasticity with decreasing temperature. You feel that both NASA and your own management are trying to solve the problem with a bureaucratic solution, when an engineering solution is called for.

3. *Thiokol management:* You must listen to your engineers, but at the same time you must please your primary customer. There is talk in Congress of awarding a second-source contract. The last thing you want to do is admit that your product is defective. NASA is pressuring you to launch. It would be very damaging for your company if a delay is blamed on your SRBs.

4. *Rockwell management:* You are concerned about the amount of ice on the pad. Analysis by your engineers does not entirely agree with that done at Houston. Like Thiokol you must satisfy your customer. You would prefer

not to launch, but are not sure that your reason to delay is good enough. Your objective is to try to convince NASA to delay without them pointing a finger at you as the cause.

Assignment D. Working in three person groups, develop a realistic procedure for making launch decisions that would have avoided the Challenger accident. Remember that the procedure must create a consensus among individuals and organizations with different objectives, backgrounds, and priorities. Part of your work will require that you develop a methodology to determine potential risks and benefits for launching the shuttle in less than ideal conditions. Remember that in the real world, personalities are often the dominant factor in a decision.

Assignment E. Working in three-person groups, consider the problems of Allan McDonald and Roger Boisjoly. Develop a strategy to convince Thiokol management and NASA management that your safety concerns are valid. Consider the points of view of all of those who are pressing to launch. Remember that management often tends to view engineers as extremely competent in a specific area, but lacking a good understanding of the big picture.

Case Study 2

Bhopal Gas Tragedy

WHAT HAPPENED AND WHY?

The Bhopal Gas Tragedy is a catastrophe that has no parallel in industrial history. In the early morning hours of December 3, 1984, a rolling wind carried a poisonous grey cloud past the walk of the Union Carbide C plant in Bhopal, Madhya Pradesh, India. An estimated 8,000 or more people died (over three times the officially announced total), people whose hopes and dreams were ironically bound up with the technology and affluence the plant symbolised. About 3,00,000 more would suffer agonising injuries from the disastrous effects of the massive poisoning while none could say if future generations would be affected. Forty tons of toxic gases were released from Carbide's Bhopal plant and spread throughout the city. The cause was the contamination of Methyl Isocyanate (MIC) storage tank No. 610 with water carrying catalytic material. The result was a nightmare that still has no end. Residents awoke to clouds of suffocating gas and began a desperate flight through the dark streets. No alarm ever sounded, no warning was given, and no evacuation plan was prepared. When victims arrived at hospitals breathless and blind, doctors did not know how to treat them since Carbide had not provided emergency information. But it was only when the sun rose the next morning that the magnitude of the devastation was clear. Dead bodies of humans and animals blocked the streets, leaves turned black, the smell of burning chilli peppers lingered in the air. Responsible estimates suggest that as many as 10,000 may have died immediately. The precise number of deaths still remains a mystery. Besides, 2,00,000 were injured and 30,000–50,000 were too ill to ever return to their jobs. This was the Hiroshima of chemical industry.

In October 1982 a mixture of MIC, chloroform and hydrochloric acid escaped from the Bhopal plant endangering the neighbouring community and injuring a few workers. This incident made very clear the potential public risks, but in spite of the insistence of Carbide officials for safety precautions, no action was taken. All this, coupled with the series of accidents that occurred in the plant and the increasingly gloomier prospects for its turnaround, served as a signal for many well-trained and experienced engineers and operators to leave the Bhopal factory in search of more secure and satisfactory employment. Between one-half and two-thirds of the skilled engineers who were fully familiar with the plant right from the project stage and certainly since the commissioning, had left the Union Carbide Bhopal establishment before the accident.

MIC in gaseous form is heavier than air and has a tendency to settle down. In this form it is subject to wind dispersal. The geographical characteristics of the area would control the dispersal. At 11 p.m. on December 2, 1984, the pressure in the tank started building up till the safety valve opened. At that time, the carbaryl plant was stated to be working. The escaping MIC was released into the atmosphere. The leakage was during 12.45 a.m.–1.30 a.m. A gentle wind slowly moved the deadly cloud over an area of about 40 sq. km, thus causing a vast destruction of life. The suggestion of senior administrators like Mr. M.N. Buch that the plant should be located in a less populated area was ignored. Before he could take any action, he was given marching orders and transferred to another post.

The issue of the danger posed by the pesticide plant to Bhopal was raised in the M.P. Assembly in December 1982. Mr. T.S. Viyogi, labour minister in the Arjun Singh government stated "A sum of Rs. 25 crore has been invested in this unit. The factory is not a small stone, which can be shifted elsewhere. There is no danger to Bhopal, nor will there ever be." Equally confident—rather overconfident—was J. Mukund, Carbide's Works Manager, when he stated, "The gas leak just can't be from my plant. The plant is shut down. Our technology just can't go wrong, we just can't have such leaks." Once it was confirmed that the leak was indeed from Union Carbide Corporation (UCC), the Chief Medical Officer denied that MIC was fatal, stressing that it was just a *minor irritant*. While the *experts* debated, people died like flies.

Senior management design and operate plants to maximize the inflow of money, while safety and maintenance are given much lower priority, especially if a plant is losing money. Cost cutting almost always means lowering safety standards and increasing the risks of a serious accident, if not a catastrophe.

Investigations, however, revealed that before the tragedy there had not been a single year when a mishap had not occurred. On various occasions inquiries were ordered and subsequently forgotten. This showed that there was something wrong in the safety standards. In addition, the following were major contributors to the disaster:

- Gradual but sustained erosion of good maintenance practices.
- Declining quality of technical training of plant personnel, especially its supervisory staff.
- Depleting inventories of vital spares.

- An indiscriminate economy drive that starved the plant of necessary capital replacement and produced general staff demoralisation.
- An exodus of some of the more experienced and able engineers and operators from the factory.
- Last but not the least, increasing undermanning of important work stations in many parts of the plant.

Together, these factors combined to cause the multiple failures that underlay the calamitous accident which occurred on the night of December 2–3, 1984. The Bhopal disaster remains the worst industrial accident in history.

ECONOMIC AND LEGAL ASPECTS

Union Carbide's operations in India go back to the beginning of this century when it began marketing its products in the country. In 1924, an assembly plant for batteries was opened in Calcutta. By 1983 Carbide had 14 plants in India manufacturing chemicals, pesticides, batteries and other products. Union Carbide's operations in India were conducted through a subsidiary, Union Carbide India, Ltd. (UCIL). The parent US Company (UCC) held 50.9% of UCIL stock. The balance of 49.1% was owned by various Indian investors. Normally, foreign investment is limited to 40% ownership of equity in Indian companies, but the Indian government waived this requirement in the case of Union Carbide because of the sophistication of its technology and the company's potential for export.

The question obviously arises: Should India throw out the multinationals? Keeping in mind the pros and cons one may say that multinationals operating in fringe areas should be given second priority as compared to the much needed technology for key sectors of Indian industry. What is vital is that the multinational should not be allowed to function except under a strict regime of environmental controls and health and safety regulations. Unfortunately, the negligence of the authorities in India matches the avariciousness of the multinationals. The negligence shown by the Madhya Pradesh Government in the context of the Bhopal gas tragedy is representative of the situation in the rest of the country.

The Bhopal plant was licensed to manufacture 5250 tons of MIC based pesticides per year. However, peak production was only 2704 tons in 1981, falling to 1657 tons in 1983. Thus the quantity of pesticides manufactured in 1983 was only 31.37% of its licensed capacity. Was the Bhopal plant used for experiments in processes for which the UCIL was not authorized? Or was the capacity of the plant being underutilized to maintain a monopolistic hold over prices?

In the first ten months of 1984, losses amounted to Rs. 5,03,39,000. Union Carbide India Limited (UCIL), was thus directed by Union Carbide Corporation (UCC) to close the plant and prepare it for sale. When no buyer was available in India, plans were made to dismantle the factory and ship it to another country. Negotiations toward this shutdown were completed by the end of November 1984. Financial losses and plans to dismantle the plant exacerbated Carbide's already negligent management practices, leading to executive decisions that directly caused the contamination of the MIC storage tank that leaked its contents over Bhopal. While saving money for both Union Carbide Corporation (UCC) and UCIL, negligent maintenance and substantial reductions of trained personnel culminated in the horrors of December 3, 1984.

By the first anniversary, on December 3, 1985, it was more than apparent to the Indian Government that Bhopal was a major problem on its hands with which it was steadily failing to cope. The victims witnessed neither speed nor selflessness not competence nor compassion from those appointed to manage and alleviate their condition. One of the most important reasons for this paralysis of action in Bhopal was the fact that the majority of the victims were poor and, in addition, from the minority community. Not all the relatives of those officially declared dead had been compensated—even if only with the nominal Rs. 10,000 set aside for the purpose. A large proportion of the victims whose monthly income was less than Rs. 500 were promised spot cash relief of Rs. 1500, but since there was already widespread corruption, the scheme was discontinued.

Within months after the disaster, the Government of India issued an ordinance appointing itself as the sole representative of the victims for any legal dealings with Union Carbide as regards compensation. The ordinance was later replaced by the Bhopal Gas Leak (Processing of Claims) Act, 1985. Armed with this power, the Government of India filed its expected suit for compensation and damages against Union Carbide in the United States District Court for the Southern District of New York. Besides filing the suit, one of its prime responsibilities was to register the claims of each and every gas victim in Bhopal. This job was never done, or rather, not with any seriousness for the next ten years. The Government set up various inquiry commissions to investigate the causes of the disaster: they remained half-hearted initiatives at best. Union Carbide, on the other hand, moved more quickly with its 'investigations': it announced by March 1985 itself, that the disaster was due to '*an act of sabotage*' by a Sikh terrorist. Then they shifted blame to a disgruntled worker. Its Indian subsidiary, Union Carbide India Ltd. (UCIL), used the excuse of the closure of the plant to reach a settlement on December 3, 1985 with its 627 retrenched workers for a final amount of US $1.8 million.

The second year after the disaster was also a turbulent year for Union Carbide since it had to defend itself against a take-over bid by a smaller company called GAF. Was there any connection between GAF and Union Carbide in the take-over drama? Was the take-over battle a put-on for public consumption? As a result of the battle, not only was Union Carbide able to divest itself assets sufficiently to file a bankruptcy claim under US laws, thus effectively blocking any order of compensation from Bhopal, if and when the suit was decreed, but GAF walked off with $ 81 million even though the take-over failed.

In addition, Union Carbide shareholders emerged richer with dividends worth more than what they had before the gas leak disaster! The gas victims figured nowhere in this scenario. To make things worse, on May 12, 1986, Judge J.F. Keenan ruled that India and not the US was the appropriate forum for the Bhopal compensation litigation. In the first pre-trial hearing in the consolidated Bhopal litigation in US federal courts, Judge Keenan asked Carbide as "a matter of fundamental human decency' to provide an interim relief payment of $5–10 million. Although contending that, according to Government of India reports, considerable relief had already been extended to the victims (some $8 million in ex-gratia payments to affected persons plus another $4 million allocated to the MP state government to cover some of its extraordinary expenses), Carbide agreed to provide $5 million for this purpose, provided a satisfactory plan of distribution and accounting of the funds was devised. For eight months, this sensitive initiative by Judge Keenan came to naught as various principals in the litigation, including Union Carbide and the Government of India, haggled over terms of reference and conditions for using the $5 million interim relief. Finally, in November 1985, an agreement was reached that the money would be channelled through the American Red Cross to the Indian Red Cross. In Bhopal itself, on the first anniversary of the disaster, no one—not even the official of the MP Government in-charge of relief for the victims—had any idea just what the Red Cross would do with the money and, certainly, none of the money had yet benefited any victims.

On December 17, 1987, District Judge Deo passed a significant order directing Union Carbide to pay Rs. 350 crores as interim relief. The order was unprecedented and decidedly controversial. Being an interim order, it could not be decreed. And without a decree UC could—and did—refuse to pay it.

Union Carbide soon challenged this order of the District Judge before the MP High Court at Jabalpur on the grounds that the trial judge was not authorized to pass the order under any provisions of the Indian Civil Penal Code. On April 4, Justice S.K. Seth of the High Court upheld the liability of Union Carbide for the Bhopal disaster but reduced the interim compensation to Rs. 250 crores and it was that order against which Union Carbide had come in appeal to the Supreme Court. For centuries before the English came here, the common law in India held a person who had injured another to pay damages, not according to the status of the victim but according to the status of the wrongdoer. That is the role of the Indian law. This law, has never been repealed. This rule of the ancient common law of India, enforced by many rulers in the last thousand years and more, is still the law of India. And it must be enforced by our courts, under the principles of justice, equity and good conscience. Then, in a shocking judgement on February 14, 1989, the Supreme Court directed Union Carbide to pay up US $470 million in "full and final settlement" of all claims, rights, and liabilities arising out of the disaster in 1984. Union Carbide was the first to describe the court's decision as fair and reasonable and the Company's stock soared in the London market immediately after the judgement. But the country as a whole, particularly the victim groups reacted in rage and with bitterness. The Bhopal Gas disaster, which left thousands of people dead and 6,00,000 injured, was settled for a mere US $470 million, which works out to around Rs. 10,000 per victim if it had been divided equally amongst all. In the same year, an article in the *Times of India* stated that approximately US $40,000 was spent on the rehabilitation of every sea otter affected by the Alaska oil spill. Each sea otter was thus given rations of lobsters costing US $500 per day. Thus the life of an Indian citizen in Bhopal was clearly much cheaper than that of a sea otter in USA.

The nation was feeling disturbed at the outcome of the case. The government which had a special responsibility in the matter had not formalized a list of the dead and injured or even got a complete compendium of the specific injuries that people had suffered. So obviously, it was premature to reach a final decision on the amount of compensation.

On September 9, 1993, Union Carbide successfully sold its entire 50.9% shares in UCIL to the Calcutta based McLeod Russell India Ltd., a company of the B.M. Khaitan Group. The shares fetched a price of Rs. 175 each, netting the Bhopal Trust a total sum of Rs. 290.23 crores. Once the hospital's total cost of Rs. 65 crores was set aside, the rest of the money would be made available to increase the settlement fund to pay compensation to the victims. Some of the money would also be used for setting up three rehabilitation centres in Bhopal.

However, even after nearly 10 years, the administration had not come to terms with the elementary fact that the money being disbursed to the gas victims was their due and not some bonus that was being doled out to them as a goodwill gesture on the part of the Government. The Claims Commissioners continued to make procedures as difficult as possible for the victims. Corruption became so rampant until in desperation once again the victims' organizations had to return to the Supreme Court.

The Bhopal scenario, even as late as 1993, presented a sordid picture. In terms of relief, the record remains disgraceful. For the most part, all that the victims received so far is the pathetic sum of Rs. 200 per month as interim relief. The Claims Courts had decided just 5% of all claims. The total compensation paid so far worked out to less than the interest earned by the Government. On the US $470 million that UCC deposited under the controversial settlement of 1989 to secure its release from all civil litigation. If Bhopal retained all its squalor despite the Rs. 216 crores that had been spent there, it was because the money had been neatly and efficiently recycled out of the pockets of the poor. The Bhopal victims have become a mere footnote to a sordid story of transfer of money from one group of vested interest—Carbide or the Government—to another: doctors, lawyers, and drug companies, many of them multinationals.

ENVIRONMENTAL ASPECT

On the night of December 2–3, 1984, a gas leak at a small pesticide plant in Central India owned by a subsidiary of Union Carbide Corporation devastated a whole city. Like natural disasters, man-made ones also seem to have a preference for the poor. Over 90% of the worst affected people were the poor living in the close vicinity of Bhopal's industrial area. They ran as fast as they could, but how could, they overtake the cars and scooters of the rich? And what is the ownership of a telephone if not the best chance that you will be warned by friends of impending disaster? The job of the police who went to localities of the poor was clearly defined: Open doors to one-room tenants; and pull out bodies five, six, seven. Anees Chisti, a journalist who witnessed the tragedy first hand states, "after a while we began to devalue the meaning of death. On seeing another dead body, all one felt was a twinge of sadness, rather like what one feels when an Indian batsman walks back to the pavilion". The Bhopal disaster which killed several thousand people and injured another two lakhs in the space of a few hours, constitutes a watershed in the history of the chemical industry.

The first of the autopsies revealed that the human blood had turned purple red, the lungs had become ash colour and filled with their own secretions. The tracheas were so dry that the mucous flaked off on touch. Sometimes the blood was so thick that if you dipped your finger in it and lifted it, it would come off like a wire.

The gas leak saw thousands blinded, breathless and giddy, flooding the hospitals, carrying those who had collapsed along the way. In cases of acute exposure, victims had suffered extensive damage to their lungs. Those who did not succumb to their injuries fell victims to secondary infections of the lungs and respiratory tracts. The psychological trauma caused by the accident is just beginning to be acknowledged and goes far beyond those physically affected by the gas. Victims suffered depression, anxiety, impotence, loss of appetite, nightmares, etc.

For one whole week the government failed to assure the citizens of Bhopal on whether the air they were breathing, the water they were drinking, and the food they were consuming were safe or not.

When the Health Department personnel were spraying DDT, some residents began to flee in panic as they imagined it was another noxious substance. On December 6, the Chief Minister declared that the air was totally safe, but tests conducted at the initiative of a group of science students indicated the presence of MIC.

Not very much is yet known about the environmental impacts of the gas leak from the Bhopal plant. The Indian Council of Agricultural Research (ICAR) had issued a preliminary report on damage to crops, vegetables, animals and fish from the accident, but the investigation reported there were mostly in their early stages with few conclusive findings.

The ICAR Report did indicate that the impact of whatever toxic substances emerge from the plant was highly lethal on exposed animals. Many were reported to have died within three minutes of such exposure. Large numbers of cattle (estimates range as high as 4000), as well as dogs and cats and birds were killed.

Plant life was also severely damaged by exposure to the gas. Vegetable crops such as spinach, cauliflower and tomatoes grown by small farmers on the outskirts of the city were destroyed. There was also widespread defoliation of trees, especially in low lying areas.

In the name of economic development, Third World countries are thus becoming dumping grounds for hazardous technologies from the industrially advanced countries. The strong environmental awareness and environmental movements in the industrially advanced countries have enforced strict legislative safeguards that have made the operation of hazardous technology economically unviable. Many pesticides that are being pushed in Third World countries by multinationals are already banned in industrially advanced countries. DDT is a typical example which is being freely overused in India. To expect strict enforcement of environmental safeguards is to forget the basic economic fact that relocation is taking place to avoid such enforcements. Statistics state that every year approximately 22,000 people die in the developing countries from the use of pesticides no longer manufactured in the West.

Conclusion

First, the tragedy was caused by the synergy of the worst of American and Indian cultures. An American corporation cynically used a third world country to escape from the increasingly strict safety standards imposed at home. Safety procedures were minimal and neither the American owners nor the local management seemed to regard them as necessary. When the disaster struck, there was no disaster plan that could be set into action. Prompt action by the local authorities could have saved many, if not most, of the victims. The immediate response was marred by callous indifference.

Secondly, we must frankly acknowledge that the legal system failed the victims and then begin to consider reforms. Our legal regime requires a radical reorientation. Given the so-called new economic policy which welcomes investments in every conceivable sector, we will see the emergence of multinationals in pursuit of cheap labour and markets. We need to introduce a system of laws which will make them accountable for higher standards of safety. We also need to see international treaties to enable the victims of any tragedy to sue these companies in the country of the origin or in their own home countries. Multinationals operating in India, must agree as a condition of doing business that they will submit to the jurisdiction of the Indian courts, both civil and criminal. They must agree to be responsible for the acts of their subsidiaries and not disown them like rats leaving a sinking ship.

The attempt by the top management of the Union Carbide, USA to shift all the blame for the Bhopal tragedy to the management of its Indian branch is churlish to say the least. At his press conference in Connecticut, Warren Anderson (President UCc) transferred the blame to India, and stated, "It is their country, their company, their people". He completely ignored the fact that the parent company owned more than 50% of the shares and thus retained the power of management. It so appeared that UC was not only grossly negligent in the design, maintenance, and operation of the plant, but equally callous in its response to the accident. The Madhya Pradesh government was all set to arrest Mr. Anderson, but was the Madhya Pradesh government less guilty? Just as UC should have had the self-realization to exercise the greatest care and take the maximum precaution when it was dealing with chemical gases as lethal as they have proved to be, it was the bounden administrative duty of the state government to play its supervisory and regulatory role with the utmost seriousness. The record shows that the state government has been no less guilty of criminal negligence. The Prime Minister Rajiv Gandhi himself made a brief appearance at the Hamidia Hospital in Bhopal and stayed just long enough to be photographed before dashing off to resume his election campaign. MNCs must accept, as a binding rule, absolute liability for their hazardous activities. In addition, all victims of personal injury must have the right to claim interim damages if they can show a prima facie case. India should consider legalizing the system of contingency peace. The sacrifice of the victims of the Bhopal tragedy will have been in vain unless some of these changes can be introduced in the law.

The dead may not have been so unlucky after all. The end came horribly, but at least the nightmare was brief. For those who survived the MIC leak, the release will not come so quickly. Thousands of the seriously affected survivors still suffer such extensive lung damage that they can no longer apply themselves physically and walking briskly even for a few minutes sends them gasping to their knees. Women have peculiar gynecological problems and are still giving birth to deformed children. Though there is need for more health care centres the funds provided by UC are grossly inadequate, and UC is reluctant to provide further finance towards the 500 bed hospital for the victims at Bhopal.

MIC in gaseous form is heavier than air and has a tendency to settle down. In this form, it is subject to wind dispersal. The geographical characteristics of the area would control the dispersal. At 11 p.m. on December 2, 1984, the pressure in the tank started building up till the safety valve opened. At that time, the carbonyl plant was stated to be working. The escaping MIC was released into the atmosphere. The leakage was between 12.45 a.m. and 01.30 a.m. A gentle wind slowly moved the deadly cloud over an area of about 40 sq. km, thus causing a vast destruction of life. The suggestion of senior administrators like Mr. M.N. Buch that the plant should be located in a less populated area was ignored. Before he could take any action he was given marching orders and transferred to another post.

This capacity of the politicians of India to capitalize positively on a tragedy for which they are partially responsible has ensured their survival while the people they are supposed to represent and take care of, die. The late Prime Minister Rajiv Gandhi himself made a brief appearance at the Hamidia Hospital in Bhopal and stayed just long enough to be photographed before dashing off to resume his election campaign. The relief that follows the tragedy is far more important for these politicians than the victims of the tragedy. All these accidents and disasters provide our politicians the much needed relief that comes from the public exchequer but is essential for the political survival. In this manner, in the absence of public accountability while individual politicians flourish, the political system collapses.

ENVIRONMENTAL IMPACT ASSESSMENT

In view of the Bhopal gas tragedy, future projects in a developing country like India must apply Environmental Impact Assessment (EIA) to fulfill the following objectives:

1. to identify adverse environmental problems that may be expected to occur;
2. to incorporate into the development action appropriate mitigation measures;
3. to identify the environmental benefits and drawbacks of the project, as well as its economic and environmental acceptability to the community;
4. to identify critical environmental problems which require further studies and/or monitoring;
5. to examine and select the optimal alternative from the various relevant options available;
6. to involve the public in the decision-making process related to the environment; and
7. to assist all parties involved in development and environmental affairs to understand their roles, responsibilities and overall relationships with one another.

Environmental Impact Assessment is essentially a preventive process which avoids costly mistakes in planning and development. Therefore, it is necessary to carry out EIA during the feasibility study stage of the planning process. India must carry out EIA for its development projects in order to ensure economic development. It should ensure rational geographic distribution of its development plans and try to avert adverse environmental impacts in the future. Training of skilled manpower and an easy access to information from other countries having somewhat similar physical and socio-economic conditions are important factors which could determine the quality of environmental assessments to be made.

Developing countries must carry out EIAs to the best of their national capability. Therefore, it is urgently necessary to train their own experts in EIA. Foreign experts are no substitute for well-trained local experts. The involvement of local expertise will not only ensure that EIAs are carried out more suited to local needs, but will also result in a significant reduction in EIA costs as compared with those conducted by foreign experts.

The need to take environmental considerations into account to ensure successful economic development is increasingly recognized throughout the world. Laws of many countries provide that reports on environmental impacts must be submitted for public review.

Environmental Impact Assessment provides an important methodology for acquiring a clear understanding of the relationship between the economy, society and environment and offers positive measures for better harmonizing the relationship between economic development and environmental protection as well as an effective means for strengthening environmental planning and management. The implementation of this system is of great significance to both economic development and environmental protection, especially in a developing country like India, with its horrendous Bhopal gas tragedy.

Case Study 3

The Three Mile Island Disaster

The accident at the Three Mile Island Unit 2 (TMI-2) nuclear power plant in Pennsylvania on March 28, 1979 was one of the most serious in the history of the U.S. nuclear industry. It not only brought to light the hazards associated with nuclear power, but also forced the industry to take a closer look at the operating procedures used at the time. What makes the TMI-2 accident such an interesting case study is the series of events which led up to the partial meltdown of the reactor core. It was a combination of human error, insufficient training, bad operating procedures, and unforeseen equipment failure that culminated in a nuclear accident that could have easily been prevented.

Timeline of Events Occurring during the Three Mile Island Disaster

Elapsed time	Event
00:00:00	**Pumps feeding water to the secondary loop shut down.** This was the first of two independent system failures that led to the near meltdown of the Three Mile Island Nuclear Reactor.
00:00:01	**Alarm sounds within the TMI control room.** At the time this alarm is disregarded by the operators.
00:00:02	**Water pressure and temperature in the reactor core rise.** The failure of the secondary loop pump has stopped the transfer of heat from the primary loop to the secondary loop. The rise in temperature and pressure is considered to be part of the normal plant operations, and hence ignored.
00:00:03	**Pressure Relief Valve (PORV) automatically opens.** When the pressure of steam in the reactor core rises above safe limits, the pressure relief valve is designed to automatically open, releasing the excess steam to a containment tank.

Cont.

Timeline of Events Occurring during the Three Mile Island Disaster
(Cont.)

Elapsed time	Event
00:00:04	**Backup pumps for the secondary loop water system automatically turn on.** Four seconds into the accident the secondary loop water pumps are automatically turned on. This is indicated to the operators by the presence of lights on the control panel. The operators are not aware that the pumps have been disconnected and are not functioning.
00:00:09	**Boron and Silver control rods are lowered into the reactor. PORV light goes out, indicating valve is closed.** Lowering of the control rods into the reactor core slows down the rate of the reaction, the effect of which is also a reduction in the heat produced by the reactor. When the PORV light goes out, the operators incorrectly assume that the valve is closed. In reality the valve is not only open but is also releasing steam and water from the core. This is now a LOCA (Loss of Coolant Accident).
00:02:00	**Emergency Injection Water (EIW) is automatically activated.** The EIW is a safety device that causes water to flow into the reactor core. It is designed to ensure that when there is a LOCA, the water in the core remains at a safe level. In the past the EIW system has turned itself on when there has been no leak so that the operators are not unduly concerned by this.
00:04:30	**Operators observe that the water level in the Primary System is rising while the pressure is decreasing.** When they observe that the water level in the core is rising the operators shut off the EIW system.
00:04:30	**Water level in the core still appears to be rising.** In actuality the water level in the core is dropping and turning off the EIW increases the amount of steam being produced by the reactor core. The combination of steam and water is still being released through the PORV.
00:08:00	**Operator notices that the valves for the secondary loop backup pumps are off.** 8 minutes into the accident the closed valve is noticed by an operator. Once he turns the valves back on the Secondary Water loop is functioning correctly.
00:45:00	**Water level in primary loop continues to drop.** At this point in the accident the operators still do not suspect a LOCA. The instrument checking the radiation has not registered an alarm, and the gauges in the control room are wrongly indicating that the water level is up.

Cont.

Timeline of Events Occurring during the Three Mile Island Disaster (Cont.)

Elapsed time	Event
01:20:00	**Primary loop pumps start to shake violently.** Steam produced by the lack of cooling water in the core passes through the primary loop pumps and causes them to shake. Assuming they are not functioning correctly, the operators turn off two of the four pumps.
01:20:00	**Remaining two pumps in the primary loop turn off.** The automatic shutdown of the two remaining pumps in the primary loop causes the water within the nuclear core to stop circulating. This in turn causes the heated core to convert more water into steam, further reducing the transfer of heat away from the core.
02:15:00	**Water level drops below the top of the core.** Once the top of the core is exposed, the steam is converted to superheated steam. This reacts with the control rods and produces hydrogen and other radioactive gases.
02:15:00	**Hydrogen gas is released through PORV.** Since the Pilot Operated Relief Valve is still in the open position it allows the hydrogen gas produced to be released along with the steam.
02:20:00	**Operator from next shift arrives and closes PORV backup valve.**
02:20:30	**Operators receive first indication that the radiation levels are up.**
02:45:00	**Radiation alarm sounds and a site emergency is declared.** At this point half the core is uncovered and the radiation level of the water in the primary loop is 350 times its normal level.
03:00:00	**Due to higher radiation levels a General Emergency is declared.** There is still confusion as to whether the core is uncovered or not. There are some that feel the temperature readings may be erroneous.
07:30:00	**Operators pump water into the primary loop and open the PORV backup valve to lower the pressure.**
09:00:00	**Hydrogen within the containment structure explodes.** The explosion is recorded by the instruments in the control room. It is dismissed as just being a spike caused by an electrical malfunction. The sound of the explosion heard is thought by some to be a ventilator damper.
15:00:00	**Primary loop pumps are turned on.** By now a large portion of the core has melted and there is still hydrogen present in the primary loop. Water from the primary loop pumps is circulated and the core temperature is finally brought under control.

DETAILED DESCRIPTION OF ACCIDENT

At 36 seconds past 4:00 a.m. on March 28, 1979, the first of a series of pumps feeding water to the steam generators at the Three Mile Island nuclear plant stopped functioning.

It was later determined that this was caused by maintenance work being done on the Number 7 Polisher at the time. The steam produced by the reactor not only runs the generators to produce electricity but also serves to cool down the reactor core, reducing the risk of a meltdown. When the flow of the water stopped, the temperature inside the reactor core increased. This caused the water inside the reactor to expand, increasing the pressure inside the pressurizer to 2200 psi, 100 psi more than the normal. As designed, the increase in pressure caused the Pilot Operated Relief Valve (PORV), to open draining the steam and water from the reactor core in to a tank on the floor.

At this point the three emergency feedwater pumps started. An operator noticed that they were running, but he did not notice that the valves on the emergency feedwater lines were closed. The panel in the control room had lights to indicate that the valves were closed, one of the lights was covered by a yellow maintenance tag, while the operator did not notice the other light.

Despite the opening of the PORV, the pressure continued to rise, 9 seconds into the accident the control rods automatically lowered as designed to halt the fission reaction. This halted the fission reaction but the latent heat of the radioactive material continued to heat the water. Even though this heat was a fraction of what is normally produced during the fission reaction, it was enough to potentially overheat the core. Thirteen seconds into the accident, the PORV should have closed since the pressure in the reactor had dropped. The light indicating that the PORV was energized (i.e. open) shut off, leading the operators to assume that the PORV was now closed. In reality, the PORV was stuck open and steam and water were escaping from the reactor. This is known as a *Loss of Coolant Accident* (LOCA).

In the first 100 minutes of the accident, almost 32,000 gallons of water, or one-third of the reactors capacity, escaped through the PORV. The accident at TMI could have been contained had either the PORV shut at this point or the operators noticed that the valve was stuck open. During the initial stages of the accident, Edward Fredrick and Craig Faust, the Control Room Operators, were present in the control room. One of the factors that added to the severity of the accident at TMI was the inadequate training of the employees at the facility. The training was the responsibility of Met Ed and Babcock & Wilcox.

Over 100 alarms went off in the control room during the first few minutes of the accident. This added to the confusion without providing any useful information to the operators. Both Faust and Fredrick dealt with the alarms to the best of their ability based on the training they had received.

Two Minutes into the accident, the pressure of the water in the reactor dropped sharply, which caused the Emergency Injection Water (EIW) to be automatically activated. This sent about 1000 gallons of water per minute into the reactor coolant system.

The falling pressure, coupled with constant reactor coolant temperature, should have alerted the operators to the LOCA. Instead, fearing that the core would have too much water, operator Fredrick turned off one of the EIW pumps, reducing the flow of water into the core to less than 100 gallons per minute.

Eight Minutes into the accident, it was discovered that the emergency feed water was not reaching the core because of the closed valves. Operator Faust proceeded to open these valves, allowing water to rush into the steam generators. It was later discovered that these valves were closed two days earlier during a routine test of the pumps. At 4:11 a.m., an alarm signalled high water in the containment building. This is the building where all the water draining from the core through the PORV is stored. This alarm by itself should have been a clear indication of a leak in the coolant system. When Fredrick was informed of this, he recommended that the sump pumps draining water to the containment building be shut off.

By about 6:15 a.m., roughly 2 hours and 15 minutes into the accident, the level of water in the reactor had dropped below the level of the core. Unknown to the operators, the core is now uncovered. It is essential that the core remain covered at all times to prevent it from overheating. Once the core overheats, the zirconium alloy of the fuel rod cladding reacts with the steam to produce hydrogen gas. This is what happened in the TMI reactor; not only is the hydrogen produced flammable, but the diminishment of the fuel rod cladding increases the risk of radioactive contamination.

The water continued to leak out of the PORV until 6:22 a.m. when Leland Rogers, the Babcock & Wilcox site representative at TMI asked the operators if they had shut the block valve which is the backup valve to the PORV. At this point the PORV was shut after having remained open for 2 hours and 22 minutes. It is still unclear whether Rogers was responsible for the valve being shut. Edward Fredrick testified that the valve was closed at the suggestion of a shift supervisor coming onto the next shift. Based on increasing radiation levels, at around 7:00 a.m., a site emergency was declared, indicating the threat of release of radioactivity into the surrounding environment. As the radiation levels continued to increase, the staff of TMI-2 was contacting local law enforcement and local energy providers. At 7:24 a general emergency was declared at the TMI-2 site, and the site began to be evacuated. By 11:00 a.m. all nonessential personnel were ordered off of the island, and the remaining technicians were forced to wear face masks to block any air-borne radioactive particles. At 1:50 p.m. the operators in the control room heard what they described as a loud "thud." While they dismissed the sound as well as the pressure spike indicated by their instruments as a malfunction, the thud was actually a hydrogen explosion inside the containment building. It was several hours, before the partially melted core could be brought to a controllable temperature using water from the primary loops.

IMMEDIATE REACTION TO THE ACCIDENT

Shortly after the accident occurred, an incorrect reading reported traces of radioactive iodine-131 in the Goldsboror area. While the reading caused an immediate need for concern, the readings were later found to be erroneous. A build-up in radioactive iodine in human's thyroids from inhaling radioactive particles or drinking contaminated milk remained the primary concern of the top officials including Governor William Scranton III. The Governor was incorrectly informed that the release of steam represented the primary concern to the surrounding environment, despite the fact that there was no indication that radioactive steam had escaped from the reactor core or the pumps feeding the core.

The evening of the accident, mayor of Goldsboror, Ken Meyers, met with his council members to discuss the possibility of an evacuation. The council members proceeded to go door to door through the town, providing families with whatever information they could, mostly consisting of information they themselves had heard from news reports, as well as explaining the evacuation procedure should Governor Scranton declare a state of emergency.

Following the accident, numerous tests were conducted in attempts to conclude what if any effect increased radiation would have on the health of human, animal and plant life in the surrounding area. Through these studies, it was revealed that the majority of radioactive material had been contained by the core. Despite the immediate concern, however, a later government report indicated that there would likely be one additional death as a result of cancer due to increased radiation levels in the surrounding area in a 30-year period.

THE CLEAN-UP OPERATION

During the clean-up operations at the Three Mile Island nuclear reactor, there were issues of ethical misconduct on the part of both organizations and individuals that occurred. Professor Stephen Unger of Columbia University has discussed one such example in his book *Controlling Technology*.

THE ISSUE

In any industrial operation, overhead cranes used for lifting heavy equipment play an important role. The polar crane used during the cleanup of TMI-2 had been damaged during the original accident. During the repairing of the crane, various parts which were damaged had been substituted with replacements that were not exactly the same as the originals. In addition, the crane, had been modified to perform duties that exceeded the original manufacturer specifications. Due to the nature of the cleanup operation, the changes made posed a hazard to not only the workers on site but also to people in the surrounding areas.

King received reports from both Parks and Gischel which stated concerns over the use of the Polar Crane. Prior to that, King had already experienced difficulties with the cleanup operations. He felt that established engineering procedures were not being followed by other high level managers, particularly Bechtel people.

Based on what he had seen and the reports he received, King decided that the crane should be carefully tested before being put into service. Top management at GPUN and Bechtel did not agree with King's assessment of the situation and felt that he was being overly cautious.

In reaction to the Gischel's report, King's superior ordered him to immediately fire Gischel. King refused and defended Gischel's position. At this point GPU's tactics turned nasty.

After suffering a stroke a year before, Gischel had seen a psychologist working under GPU. At the time, the psychologist suggested he take a neuropsychological evaluation, but he refused to take the test. Almost immediately following the release of the report, he again received a letter suggesting he take the test. Robert Arnold, the President of GPU Nuclear, continued pressuring Gischel and, in a clear violation of the doctor-patient relationship, disclosed that he had knowledge of the topics of Gischel's meetings with the GPU employed psychologist. After a letter from the Board Chairman of GPU, insisting Gischel take the exam Gischel sent a sworn affidavit to Arnold explaining his take on the TMI cleanup operations and the events that followed. Gischel requested that Arnold forward the affidavit to the NRC which he did, but on July 1 after Gischel still refused to take the neuropsychological exam, he was transferred to a different subsidiary of GPU.

Richard Parks also filed a sworn affidavit and submitted it to the NRC, and a harassment complaint filed against GPU Nuclear. Parks's complaint was filed on the grounds that a manager told him Parks's superiors were considering transferring him off site, he was demoted from his position as alternate startup and test manager, and was informed of a false rumour that his ex-wife (who was actually deceased) was trying to dig up dirt on Parks to get custody of their two children. The day after he filed his complaint, Parks was suspended with pay on the grounds that his continued working would subject him to continued harassment from his co-workers.

In February of 1983, GPU Nuclear accused King of hiring employees away from GPUN for his own firm, Quiltec. Accused of a conflict of interest, King was suspended and locked out of his office while he claims that documents he wrote concerning the cleanup process were destroyed. King's secretary,

Joyce Wagner, was also forced into suspension and within a month both king and Wagner had been fired.

THE IMPACT OF ACCIDENT

The numerous ethical questions surrounding the TMI-2 cleanup procedure might suggest that nothing positive could have resulted from the incident. Beyond the questionable behaviour on the part of the companies responsible for the cleanup, radiation presented a major problem for the cleanup crews as did algae that not only grew, but thrived in the contaminated water. There were important scientific as well as sociological issues that resulted from the accident. The following is based on Matthew L. Wald's article "After the Meltdown, Lessons from a Cleanup" that appeared in the April 24, 1990 edition of the *New York Times*.

What the clean-up effort did prove was that, despite requiring 400 workers, over 4 1/2 years, and 970 million dollars, the cleanup of a nuclear disaster area is still possible. Unlike the Soviet approach to the cleanup at the Chernobyl disaster site, where the reactor was encased in an enormous concrete structure, the cleanup of the reactor site and, especially the reactor vessel at TMI-2, provided many answers to questions surrounding the accident, and even provided some hints as to the nature of exactly how stable reactor vessels are.

During the cleanup process, the team learned that despite the 51% meltdown of the reactor core, that the reactor vessel was relatively undamaged. This indicated two separate points. First that it was far easier to have a meltdown to the core than expected, but secondly that at least in this case, the reactor vessel was able to withstand temperature much higher than anticipated.

Beyond scientific impact, however, remains the impact that the accident had on the public. Many analysts in the nuclear industry believe that the incident at TMI-2 has meant the nuclear industry has only one more chance. Analysts feel that another nuclear accident on the scale of TMI-2 will result in public outcry for the closing of the other nuclear plants around the nation.

NUCLEAR REACTOR TECHNICAL INFORMATION

It is important to understand the basics of how a nuclear reactor produces electricity and what the basic components of the reactor at Three Mile Island were. Three Mile Island was the home to two nuclear plants, TMI-1 and TMI-2. Their combined power generating capacity was 1,700 megawatts, or enough electricity to supply 300,000 homes. In a nutshell, nuclear power plants generate electricity by using steam turbines. The function of the nuclear fuel is to heat water and convert it to steam. Now in theory this sounds quite simple, but the hazards associated with nuclear fuels add to the complications. A nuclear reactor such as TMI-2 can be divided into various sub-systems.

The Nuclear Reactor
Water Systems—Primary Water Loop (Reactor Coolant Loop) — Secondary Water Loop (Feedwater System)—Condenser Water
Steam Generators
Steam Turbine
Auxiliaries—Water Pumps, Pressurizer
In order to understand the accident at TMI, it is essential that we have a rudimentary understanding of how these systems function.

THE NUCLEAR REACTOR

A nuclear reactor generates heat by harnessing atomic energy. The core of an atom, which is also called the nucleus, can be split by bombarding it with neutrons. When a free neutron strikes the core, it splits the atom into two smaller atom fragments, giving off energy in the form of kinetic energy of the fragments, plus two or three neutrons, and probably, some gamma rays: One of the neutrons produced by this reaction strikes another atom, which in turn produces more energy and more neutrons. This chain reaction continues from one atom to another producing nuclear fission energy[1].

The TMI-2 Reactor Core held 100 tons of uranium to fuel the nuclear reaction. This was in the form of cylindrical uranium oxide pellets that were one inch tall and roughly one half inch wide. These pellets were stacked inside 12-foot long fuel rods made of a zirconium alloy (Zircaloy-4). The entire reactor consisted of 36,816 such fuel rods along with 69 control rods, 52 instrument tubes and spaces between them for the cooling water to flow.

Control rods are used to control the amount of power produced by the reactor, or to completely halt the reaction in case of an emergency. The control rods are able to control the rate of nuclear fission taking place by absorbing a portion of the free neutrons produced. The rate varies depending on the number of rods and the length of the rod inserted into the core of the reactor. TMI-2 used control rods made of 80% Silver, 15% indium, and 5% cadmium.

Control rods are designed such that in the event of an emergency the magnetic clamps holding them release the rods into the core of the reactor, thus completely halting the reaction.

The Instrument Tubes contain instruments used to measure such things as the temperature within the reactor.

WATER SYSTEMS

There are three basic closed-loop Water Systems in a nuclear power plant, such as the one at TMI.

The first water system is the Primary Loop or the Reactor Coolant System. This is a closed loop system that circulates water through the nuclear core and serves two purposes. First, by coming in contact with the hot fuel rods the water is heated. At the same time the water flowing through the core cools down the fuel rods, preventing them from melting. It is important that the water coming in contact with the reactor core remain in liquid form so that it can effectively cool the rods. In order to prevent the water from turning into steam, it is pressurized to about 2,155 psi. In the event of an accident, either an increase in temperature or a decrease in pressure can convert the heated water to steam. This is undesirable but not dangerous because the steam too can help cool the reactor core.

Once the steam from the Feedwater System has driven the turbines, it goes to the condenser where it is cooled and converted back to water. The final water system is the Condenser Water that is cooled in the cooling towers. This is the water used to cool the steam from the turbines and is also a closed loop water system. This ensures that the radioactive water from the reactor cannot contaminate the water in the cooling towers or the water vapour that is released from the cooling towers to the atmosphere.

Under normal operating conditions, the primary loop is the only system that contains traces of radiation.

STEAM GENERATORS

Heated water from the reactor goes to the Steam Generator where it is passed through corrosion resistant tubes. At the same time, water from the Secondary Loop or Feedwater System is passed through the steam generator around the tubes containing hot water from the reactor. This converts the Secondary Loop water into steam and also cools down the reactor coolant water. It is important to note that at no point does water from the two separate systems mix with each other.

STEAM TURBINE

The steam is then sent to the Steam Turbines where it runs the electricity-producing generator while the relatively cooler water of the Reactor Coolant System is sent back into the reactor core to pick up more heat and repeat the whole cycle.

AUXILIARIES

The Pressurizer ensures that the reactor coolant water is kept at the correct pressure. If for some reason the water pressure increases above safe levels, the Pilot Operated Relief Valve (PORV) is supposed to open, thus relieving excess pressure by releasing water/steam to the drain tank. While this solves the immediate problem and prevents the reactor vessel from getting damaged, it reduces the level of water in nuclear core.

A reduction in the reactor core water level would lead to the core being uncovered. This is undesirable because it would allow the core temperature to increase beyond safe levels. If the core temperature were to reach around 2,200 degrees Fahrenheit the water would begin to react with the cladding producing hydrogen. This could potentially explode. If the temperature were to reach 5,200 degrees Fahrenheit, the uranium could potentially melt, releasing far more radioactive materials into the surroundings.

Case Study 4

The Chernobyl Disaster

A recent article in the Express on Saturday, March 6, 1999 identifies the potential for another nuclear disaster at the Chernobyl Power Station. The final reactor at the plant has just been turned back on after repairs, but at the turn of the century the environmental disaster that happened in 1986, could be repeated due to the potential problem that is the millennium bug.

Sergei Parachin, head of the pressure group Energy and Computer Science for the 21st Century claimed that top officials at the plant were ignoring the potential dangers of the millennium bug at the aging nuclear plant. The meltdown in 1986 left many dead as a result of subsequent radiation leaks as well as the initial accident. This was the world's worst civilian atomic disaster.

Authorities claim that their energy sector is not fully computerized, and is fairly 'low-tech', but Parachin claims that they do not fully understand the problem. There is a possibility that at the turn of the millennium the reactor could simply shut down causing meltdown similar to the 1986 event. (The picture right illustrates an 'elephant's foot' caused by the melting of the protective shell of the reactor core). This could lead to a disaster at the turn of the century that could be far more severe than the previous event. Millennium meltdown would not be the result of a test gone wrong, and would therefore not only affect the Chernobyl reactor, but other ageing nuclear plants in the Ukraine.

It is not just the Ukrainian reactors that could potentially release radioactive material, it could be other Russian designed plants across Europe. The thumbnail illustrates the extent of nuclear reactors across Europe, both Russian designed and other plants.

If there is an incident at the turn of the millennium, then it would produce similar problems to the 1986 meltdown, but on a potentially larger scale.

These are the topics that are covered in this case study:

The effect of another Chernobyl disaster in the year 2000 would be great, and the radiation from a meltdown could affect not just the local people within the area of the meltdown, but people Europe-wide, and possibly World-wide.

In 1986 the radiation cloud that leaked from Chernobyl affected many people in Europe. This table shows the doses obtained in some European countries and the 50-year exposure figures (U.S. estimates) taken from soil samples.

Country	**Collective effective Dose Alltime NRBP estimates**	**50-yr Dose (man-Sv or Person-Gy) American Estimates**
Belgium	940	880
Denmark	1,100	820
France	5,600	12,000
Federal Republic of Germany	30,000	58,000
Greece	8,500	4,700
Ireland	950	1,800
Italy	27,000	52,000
Luxembourg	42	76
Netherlands	1,200	3,400
Portugal	2.3	Low
Spain	57	Low
U.K.	3,000	15,000

In 1986 the Rural Population within the Zhitomir Province in the Ukraine, both adults and children were greatly affected by the meltdown. There was an increase in heart disease from 518 sufferers in 1986, to 757 in 1987, 807 in 1988 and 430 in the first quarter of 1989.

The official toll for the disaster was 3,576 dead, and 40,000 disabled. However, these figures are possibly higher, as 15,000 of the 60,000 people who were involved in the clean-up operation are now dead.

A much larger number of people were thought of as being significantly exposed to radiation.

If an event occurs due to the millennium bug in Chernobyl and/or other similar reactors, then these figures could be much higher. If more than one station is affected, then radiation could affect the whole of Europe, and could potentially affect people throughout the World.

Problems that would arise from meltdowns, potentially across Europe would be seen globally. Main contamination would be in countries immediately in the vicinity to the meltdown sites. In 1986, the major hotspots were all located around the Ukraine. The rural areas were worst affected in the former Russian states. These were once fertile areas that could be farmed. These areas are now too contaminated to grow anything. These local rural populations were forced to move out of these contaminated areas, and the areas they were moved to did not guarantee permanent subsidized housing. There were over

1,00,000 rural evacuees in areas close to the Ukraine. The first affected country other than the Ukraine was Belarus to the north.

The plume of radiation also had immediate effects on the Nordic countries. The radiation at this time was around 20–150 counts per second (normal range in 5–10 counts per second). Scientist at Studsvik identified 16 radio nuclides within the radiation cloud, some of which showed readings >1000 counts per second. This first identified that there had been a meltdown, as one of the radio nuclides was Ruthenium, which melts at 2250°C!

Of all of the Nordic countries, Sweden was the worst affected, with contamination of meat and lichen. Meat from 50,000 reindeer had to be thrown away. The lichen, which is used as a food source contained up to 30,000 Bq/kg. Altogether, the effects to Sweden totalled $100 million in the first year alone. The fallout in Sweden also caused around 100 more fatalities due to cancer derived from high doses of radiation.

Problems arose in the USA due to fallout along with most of the Northern Hemisphere. In Britain meat from many animals such as sheep was marked 'inedible' due to fallout from the Chernobyl leak.

A millennium bug induced meltdown across all of the Ukraine's nuclear plants, and other plants in Europe would have more wide reaching consequences. The grazing livestock of many more countries in the Northern Hemisphere would be contaminated with radiation. This could even spread into the Southern Hemisphere due to a much larger plume of radiation. The cost of the contamination of all foodstuffs including crops and vegetables could be enormous, causing huge agricultural problems across the globe at the turn of the millennium'.

The major effects of a nuclear meltdown in the year 2000 would be the global spread of radiation. Immediate effects would include the damage to agriculture in Europe, particularly Eastern Europe. The EU would be forced to place a ban on all agricultural goods from countries it thought were sufficiently affected. This would cause the breakdown of the agricultural community, as trade in these goods would cease locally, and exports would be banned. This would lead to increased cost for imported goods at a cost to the local consumer, who wouldn't have money to spend due to him/her being unable to sell their own goods.

The main factor that affected was the plume of smoke and debris that travelled through Europe. The cloud passed through eastern parts of Poland and parts of the former Federal Republic of Germany. Most of the contamination across Europe was caused by fallout from the plume. The thumbnail shows the pattern the plume took across Europe. Within 10 days of the meltdown, the cloud had travelled across the globe.

If this incident was repeated by a millennium bug induced reactor leak from all of the Ukraine's nuclear plants, as well as other Russian built plants across Europe, the spread of the cloud could be much quicker, and cover a greater area.

Appendix 1

Institution of Engineers (India)
Sample Codes of Ethics

Preamble

To uphold the concept of the professional conduct amongst the corporate members, the Institution of Engineers (India) introduced the professional Conduct Rules on August 30, 1944 which was replaced by the code of ethics from October 15, 1954. This was again revised on August 12, 1962. Consistent with the changing needs of the profession, the Council of the I.E.I. again revised the Code of Ethics for corporate members in its meeting held on June 29, 1997.

Ethics deals with moral duty and obligation and gives rise to a set of values which in turn are used to judge the appropriateness of particular conduct or behaviour. These are the basic principles with which the members are to be guided in their daily professional work and decision making.

The Code is based on broad principles of truth, honesty, justice and trustworthiness, and respect and safeguard of human life and welfare, competence and accountability, which constitute the values every member must recognize and uphold.

CODE OF ETHICS FOR CORPORATE MEMBERS

A corporate member shall —

(a) Practice his profession with integrity, conscience, dignity and honour and follow the best traditions of the profession.

(b) Be aware that the principles of ecosystemic interdependence, diversity maintenance, resource recovery and inter–relational harmony form the basis of our continued existence and that each of these poses a threshold of sustainability that should not be exceeded.

(c) Hold paramount the safety, health and welfare of the people and the protection of the environment and promote health and safety within the work place.

(d) Offer services, advice on or undertake engineering assignments only in the areas of his competence and furnish correct information of his qualifications and experience to concerned clients.

(e) Uphold and maintain confidentiality and respect for secrets confided in him by the clients, employers and employees in connection with any professional work undertaken by him.

(f) Keep informed and updated in his area of professional activity and strive to provide opportunities for professional developments of his subordinates.

(g) Conduct, without consideration of caste, creed, sect, social status, and shall not perform and act against the interest of the nation.

(h) Present clearly to all concerned, the possible consequences of ignoring, overruling or discarding technological and engineering decisions or judgements without proper justification.

(i) Not directly or indirectly injure the professional reputation of another corporate member.

(j) Not accept any unauthorized commission, discount, allowance or profit, direct or indirect, to himself in connection with any work under his charge or for any professional business entrusted to him.

(k) Not act in a manner which may injure the reputation or the image of the institution or may cause damage to the institution financially or otherwise.

Appendix 2

ACM Code of Ethics and Professional Conduct

Preamble

Commitment to ethical professional conduct is expected of every member (voting members, associate members, and student members) of the Association for Computing Machinery (ACM).

The Code shall be supplemented by a set of Guidelines, which provide explanation to assist members in dealing with the various issues contained in the Code. It is expected that the Guidelines will be changed more frequently than the Code.

The Code and its supplemented Guidelines are intended to serve as a basis for ethical decision making in the conduct of professional work. Secondarily, they may serve as a basis for judging the merit of a formal complaint pertaining to violation of professional ethical standards.

It should be noted that, although computing is not mentioned in the imperatives, the Code is concerned with how these fundamental imperatives apply to one's conduct as a computing professional. These imperatives are expressed in a general form to emphasize that ethical principles which apply to computer ethics are derived from more general ethical principles.

It is understood that, some words and phrases in a code of ethics are subject to varying interpretations, and that any ethical principle may conflict with other ethical principles in specific situations. Questions related to ethical conflicts can best be answered by thoughtful consideration of fundamental principles, rather than reliance on detailed regulations.

GENERAL MORAL IMPERATIVES

1. Contribute to society and human well-being. This principle concerning the quality of life of all people affirms an obligation to protect fundamental human rights and to respect the diversity of all cultures. An essential aim of computing professionals is to minimize negative consequences of computing systems, including threats to health and safety. When designing or implementing systems, computing professionals must attempt to ensure that the products of their efforts will be used in socially responsible ways, will meet social needs, and will avoid harmful effects to health and welfare.

In addition to a safe social environment, human well-being includes a safe natural environment. Therefore, computing professionals who design and develop systems must be alert to, and make others aware of, any potential damage to the local or global environment.

2. Avoid harm to others. "Harm" means injury or negative consequences, such as undesirable loss of information, loss of property, property damage, or unwanted environmental impacts. This principle prohibits use of computing technology in ways that result in harm to any of the following: users, the general public, employees, and employers. Harmful actions include intentional destruction or modification of files and programs, leading to serious loss of resources or unnecessary expenditure of human resources such as the time and effort required to purge systems of "computer viruses."

Well-intended actions, including those that accomplish assigned duties, may lead to harm unexpectedly. In such an event, the responsible person or persons are obligated to undo or mitigate the negative consequences as much as possible. One way to avoid unintentional harm is to carefully consider potential impacts on all those affected by decisions made during design and implementation.

To minimize the possibility of indirectly harming others, computing professionals must minimize malfunctions by following generally accepted standards for system design and testing. Furthermore, it is often necessary to assess the social consequences of systems to project the likelihood of any serious harm to others. If system features are misrepresented to users, coworkers, or supervisors, the individual computing professional is responsible for any resulting injury.

In the work environment, the computing professional has the additional obligation to report any signs of system dangers that might result in serious personal or social damage. If one's superiors do not act to curtail or mitigate such dangers, it may be necessary to 'blow the whistle' to help correct the problem or reduce the risk. However, capricious or misguided reporting of violations can, itself, be harmful. Before reporting violations, all relevant aspects of the incident must be thoroughly assessed. In particular, the assessment of risk and responsibility must be credible. It is suggested that advice be sought from other computing professionals.

3. Be honest and trustworthy. Honesty is an essential component of trust. Without trust an organization cannot function effectively. The honest computing professional will not make deliberately false or deceptive claims about a system or system design, but will instead provide full disclosure of all pertinent system limitations and problems.

A computer professional has a duty to be honest about his or her own qualifications, and about any circumstances that might lead to conflicts of interest.

Membership in volunteer organizations such as ACM may at times place individuals in situations where their statements or actions could be interpreted as carrying the 'weight' of a larger group of professionals. An ACM member will exercise care in such a manner that he does not misrepresent ACM or the positions and policies of ACM, or any ACM units.

4. Be fair and take action not to discriminate. The values of equality, tolerance, respect for others, and the principles of equal justice govern this imperative. Discrimination on the basis of race, sex, religion, age, disability, national origin, or other such factors is an explicit violation of ACM policy and will not be tolerated.

Inequities between different groups of people may result from the use or misuse of information and technology. In a fair society, all individuals would have equal opportunity to participate in, or benefit from, the use of computer resources regardless of race, sex, religion, age, disability, national origin or other such similar factors. However, these ideals do not justify unauthorized use of computer resources, nor do they provide an adequate basis for violation of any other ethical imperatives of this code.

5. Honour property rights including copyrights and patent. Violation of copyrights, patents, trade secrets and the terms of license agreements is prohibited by law in most circumstances. Even when software is not so protected, such violations are contrary to professional behaviour. Copies of software should be made only with proper authorization. Unauthorized duplication of materials must not be condoned.

6. Give proper credit for intellectual property. Computing professionals are obligated to protect the integrity of intellectual property. Specifically, one must not take credit for other's ideas or work, even in cases where the work has not been explicitly protected by copyright, patent, etc.

7. Respect the privacy of others. Computing and communication technology enables the collection and exchange of personal information on a scale unprecedented in the history of civilization. Thus there is increased potential for violating the privacy of individuals and groups. It is the responsibility of professionals to maintain the privacy and integrity of data describing individuals. This includes taking precautions to ensure the accuracy of data, as well as protecting it from unauthorized access or accidental disclosure to inappropriate individuals. Furthermore, procedures must be established to allow individuals to review their records and correct inaccuracies.

This imperative implies that only the necessary amount of personal information be collected in a system, that retention and disposal periods for that information be clearly defined and enforced, and that personal information gathered for a specific purpose not be used for other purposes without consent of the individual(s). These principles apply to electronic communications, including electronic mail, and prohibit procedures that capture or monitor electronic user data, including messages, without the permission of users or bona fide authorization related to system operation and maintenance. User data observed during the normal duties of system operation and maintenance must be treated with strictest confidentiality, except in cases where it is an evidence for the violation of law, organizational regulations, or the Code. In these cases, the nature or contents of that information must be disclosed only to proper authorities.

8. Honour confidentiality. The principle of honesty extends to issues of confidentiality of information whenever one has made an explicit promise to honour confidentiality or, implicitly, when private information not directly related to the performance of one's duties becomes available. The ethical concern is to respect all obligations of confidentiality to employers, clients, and users unless discharged from such obligations by requirements of the law or other principles of the Code.

MORE SPECIFIC PROFESSIONAL RESPONSIBILITIES

1. Strive to achieve the highest quality, effectiveness and dignity in both the process and products of professional work. Excellence is perhaps the most important obligation of a professional. The computing professional must strive to achieve quality and to be cognizant of the serious negative consequences that may result from poor quality in a system.

2. Acquire and maintain professional competence. Excellence depends on individuals who take responsibility for acquiring and maintaining professional competence. A professional must participate in setting standards for appropriate levels of competence and strive to achieve those standards. Upgrading technical knowledge and competence can be achieved in several ways: doing independent study; attending seminars, conferences, or courses; and being involved in professional organizations.

3. Know and respect existing laws pertaining to professional work. ACM members must obey existing local, state, province, national, and international laws unless there is a compelling ethical basis not to do so. Policies and procedures of the organizations in which one participates must also be obeyed. But compliance must be balanced with the recognition that sometimes existing laws and rules may be immoral or inappropriate and, therefore, must be challenged. Violation of a law or regulation may be ethical when that law or rule has inadequate moral basis or when it conflicts with another law judged to be more important. If one decides to violate a law or rule because it is viewed as unethical, or for any other reason, one must fully accept responsibility for one's actions and for the consequences.

4. Accept and provide appropriate professional review. Quality professional work, especially in the computing profession, depends on professional reviewing and critiquing. Whenever appropriate, individual members should seek and utilize peer review as well as provide critical review of the work of others.

5. Give comprehensive and thorough evaluations of computer systems and their impacts, including analysis of possible risks. Computer professionals must strive to be perceptive, thorough and, objective when evaluating, recommending, and presenting system descriptions and alternatives. Computer professionals are in a position of special trust and therefore, have a special responsibility to provide objective, credible evaluations to employers, clients, users, and the public. When providing evaluations, the professional must also identify any relevant conflicts of interest.

6. Honour contracts, agreements, and assigned responsibilities. Honouring one's commitments is a matter of integrity and honesty. For the computer professional, this includes ensuring that system elements perform as intended. Also, when one contracts for work with another party, one has an obligation to keep that party properly informed about progress toward completing that work.

A computing professional has a responsibility to request a change in any assignment that he or she feels cannot be completed as defined. Only after serious consideration and with full disclosure of risks and concerns to the employer or client, should one accept the assignment. The major underlying principle here is the obligation to accept personal accountability for professional work. On some occasions other ethical principles may take greater priority.

A judgement that a specific assignment should not be performed may not be accepted. Having clearly identified one's concerns and reasons for that judgement, but failing to procure a change in that assignment, one may yet be obligated, by contract or by law, to proceed as directed. The computing professional's ethical judgement should be the final guide in deciding whether or not to proceed. Regardless of the decision, one must accept the responsibility for the consequences. However, performing assignments "against one's own judgement" does not relieve the professional of responsibility for any negative consequences.

7. Improve public understanding of computing and its consequences. Computing professionals have a responsibility to share technical knowledge with the public by encouraging understanding of computing, including the impacts of computer systems and their limitations. This imperative implies an obligation to counter any false views related to computing.

8. Access computing and communication resources only when authorized to do so. Theft or destruction of tangible and electronic property is prohibited by the principle, "avoid harm to others." Trespassing and unauthorized use of a computer or communication system is addressed by this imperative. Trespassing includes accessing communication networks and computer systems, or accounts and/or files associated with those systems, without explicit authorization to do so. Individuals and organizations have the right to restrict access to their systems so long as they do not violate the discrimination principle. No one should enter or use another's computer system, software, or data files without permission. One must always have appropriate approval before using system resources, including communication ports, file space, other system peripherals, and computer time.

ORGANIZATIONAL LEADERSHIP IMPERATIVES

Background Note

This section draws extensively from the draft IFIP Code of Ethics, especially its sections on organizational ethics and international concerns. The ethical obligations of organizations tend to be neglected in most codes of professional conduct, perhaps because these codes are written from the perspective of the individual member. This dilemma is addressed by stating these imperatives from the perspective of the organizational leader. In this context "leader" is viewed as any organizational member who has leadership or educational responsibilities. These imperatives generally may apply to organizations as well as their leaders. In this context "organizations" are corporations, government agencies, and other "employers," as well as volunteer professional organizations.

1. Articulate social responsibilities of members of an organizational unit and encourage full acceptance of those responsibilities. Because organizations of all kinds have impacts on the public, they must accept responsibilities to society. Organizational procedures and attitudes oriented toward quality and the welfare of society will reduce harm to members of the public, thereby serving public interest and fulfilling social responsibility. Therefore, organizational leaders must encourage full participation in meeting social responsibilities as well as quality performance.

2. Manage personnel and resources to design and build information systems that enhance the quality of working life. Organizational leaders are responsible for ensuring that computer systems enhance, not degrade, the quality of working life. When implementing a computer system, organizations must consider the personal and professional development, physical safety, and human dignity of all workers. Appropriate human computer ergonomic standards should be considered in system design and in the workplace.

3. Acknowledge and support proper and authorized uses of an organization's computing and communication resources. Because computer systems can become tools to harm as well as to benefit an organization, the leadership has the responsibility to clearly define appropriate and inappropriate uses of organizational computing resources. While the number and scope of such rules should be minimal, they should be fully enforced when established.

4. Ensure that users and those who will be affected by a system have their needs clearly articulated during the assessment and design of requirements; later the system must be validated to meet requirements. Current system users, potential users and other persons whose lives may be affected by a system must have their needs assessed and incorporated in the statement of requirements. System validation should ensure compliance with those requirements.

5. Articulate and support policies that protect the dignity of users and others affected by a computing system. Designing or implementing systems that deliberately or inadvertently demean individuals or groups is ethically unacceptable. Computer professionals who are in decision making positions should verify that systems are designed and implemented to protect personal privacy and enhance personal dignity.

6. Create opportunities for members of the organization to learn the principles and limitations of computer systems. This complements the imperative on public understanding Educational opportunities are essential to facilitate optimal participation of all organizational members. Opportunities must be available to all members to help them improve their knowledge and skills in computing, including courses that familiarize them with the consequences and limitations of particular types of systems. In particular, professionals must be made aware of the dangers of building systems around oversimplified models, the improbability of anticipating and designing for every possible operating condition, and other issues related to the complexity of this profession.

COMPLIANCE WITH THE CODE

Uphold and promote the principles of the code. The future of the computing profession depends on both technical and ethical excellence. Not only is it important for ACM computing professionals to adhere to the principles expressed in the Code, each member should encourage and support adherence by other members.

Treat violations of the code as inconsistent with membership in the ACM. Adherence of professionals to a code of ethics is largely a voluntary matter. However, if a member does not follow the code by engaging in gross misconduct, membership in ACM may be terminated.

The ACM Code and the supplemental Guidelines were developed by the Task Force for the Revision of the ACM Code of Ethics and Professional Conduct: Ronald E. Anderson, Chair, Gerald Engel, Donald Gotterbarn, Grace C. Hertlein, Alex Hoffman, Bruce Jawer, Deborah G. Johnson, Doris K. Lidtke, Joyce Currie Little, Dianne Martin, Donn B. Parker, Judith A. Perrolle, and Richard S. Rosenberg. The Task Force was organized by ACM/SIGCAS, and funding was provided by the ACM SIG Discretionary Fund. This Code and the supplemental Guidelines were adopted by the ACM Council on October 16, 1992.

REFERENCES

Alan D. Wilcox, *Engineering Design for Electrical Engineers*, Prentice Hall, Englewood Cliffs, NJ, 1990.

Charles B. Fleddermann, *Engineering Ethics,* Pearson Education, New Delhi, 2004.

Charlers E. Harris, Jr., Michael S. Pritchard, and Michael J. Rabins, *Engineering Ethics: Concepts and cases*, Wadsworth Publishing Co., Belmount, California, 2000.

James Armstrong, Ross Dixon, and Simon Robinson, *The Decision Makers,* Thomas Telford, London, 1999.

Mike W. Martin and Roland Schinzinger, *Ethics in Engineering*, 3rd ed., Tata McGraw-Hill, New Delhi, 2003.

Roland Schinzinger and Mike W. Martin, *Introduction to Engineering Ethics*, McGraw-Hill, New York, 2000.

WEB RESOURCES

A list of important web sites on Ethics is given below.

1. www.ethicsandbusiness.org/whoweare.htm
2. http://ethics.acused.edu/values/index.html
3. www.lockheedmartin.com/about/ethics.html
4. www.ti.com/corp/docs/company/citizen/ethics/benchmark.shtml
5. www.ethics.ubc.ca/resources/business/
6. www.iit.edu/departments/csep/PublicWWWcodes/
7. www.ibe.org.uk/
8. www.globalethics.org/links.html
9. www.ethicsandbusiness.org/stylequiz.htm
10. http://www.scu.edu/SCU/Centers/Ethics
11. http://essential.org
12. http://violet.berkeley.edu/
13. http://www.corpwatch.org
14. http://www.worldwatch.org
15. http://www.arq.co.uk/ethicalbusiness
16. http://scuish.scu.edu/Ethics
17. http://condor.depaul.edu/ethics
18. http://www5.fullerton.edu/les/ethics list.html
19. http://www.srbnet.org
20. http://www.businessethics.org
21. http://www.essential.org
22. http://www.efund.com/investors action.html
23. http://www.envirolink.com
24. http.//www.law.indiana.edu

Index